SO YOU THINK YOU'RE A
NEW YORK YANKEES
FAN?

HOWIE KARPIN

SPORTS
PUBLISHING

Dedicated to the late Bill Shannon who was widely considered the "best Official Scorer in the country." He was also my mentor who helped jump start my career. Bill was the scorer for many of the games mentioned in this book. Thanks to him, so was I.

Contents

Introduction

What is trivia?

The word "trivia" is defined in the dictionary as "matters of things that are very unimportant, inconsequential, or nonessential."

With their long and glorious history, the New York Yankees provide a wealth of "things that are very unimportant" in the "real" world, but which are very important when it comes to understanding the legacy and the impact of the most famous sports team in the world.

Yankees history transcends sports. Lou Gehrig's memorable farewell speech on July 4, 1939, is a bookmark date in American history. In the time of the Great Depression in the 1920s, Babe Ruth was making headlines with his home-run hitting exploits, despite the despair and hard times that were enveloping the country.

This collection of trivia questions will make it fun to raise your curiosity about the history that took place, and provides the "inconsequential" answers to these "very unimportant" questions.

Over the years, many books have been written detailing the famous events and achievements that have thrilled fans throughout the history of the New York Yankees. *So You Think You're a New York Yankees Fan?* provides challenging questions about everything from historic games to less publicized, but notable, events. Then the answers provide insightful and enlightening anecdotes about the time-honored roster of all-time greats and also-rans who had their moment in the sun.

Since they came into existence in 1913, the Yankees have been an integral part of the fabric of American sports. The questions within this book range from the early days of the franchise right up to the present day, covering a lot of winning moments and some crushing defeats.

The 1927 Yankees were tagged with the famous nickname of "Murderers' Row," but can you name the starting lineup? Who threw the "folly floater?" These questions are just a small sample of the ones you will have to answer if you're to success-fully navigate your way through this book.

We hope you have as much fun in trying to solve them as we had in putting them together.

"Play ball."

ROOKIE LEVEL

(Answers begin on page 7.)

Okay "rook," we'll make it easy to get started.

A couple of "cookies" for you rookies, to get you on a roll as you head down the basepaths of this book. You can take a swing at Yankees history both old and as recent as 2016. When you get on base with a couple of right answers, make the turn at first and see if you've made the "All-Stars" in the next chapter.

1. The longest game in Yankees history lasted 22 innings. Who hit a two-run homer to win the game, and how many hours did it take to play the game?

2. Name the Yankees player who made history by becoming baseball's first designated hitter in 1973.

3. Who caught the final out of the 1962 World Series?

4. In October of 1974, the Yankees and San Francisco Giants swung a blockbuster one-for-one trade. Name the players who were involved in that memorable deal.

5. Who is the winningest manager in Yankees history?

6. In December 1992, the Yankees completed a four-player trade with the California Angels to acquire this starting pitcher. What was his name?

7. Who caught Dave Righetti's no-hitter in 1983?

8. Who was the first Yankee to win the American League Rookie of the Year Award?

9. Babe Ruth hit a total of 714 home runs, including 659 with the Yankees. Match the numbers in the right column with the correct stat he accumulated as a Yankee:

Stolen Bases   106

Caught Stealing   35

Triples   117

Runs Batted In   1,852

Base on Balls   1,978

Strikeouts   1,122

Hit by Pitch   110

10. Name the only Yankee to hit for the cycle three times.

11. In what year did Elston Howard become the Yankees' first African-American player?

12. Name the Yankees rookie who hit 11 home runs in his first 23 major league games.

13. How many times have the Yankees scored at least 20 runs in a game?

14. In their history, the Yankees' pitchers have tossed 10 regular season no-hit games. How many were at Yankee Stadium?

15. How many World Series did the Yankees win before Babe Ruth joined the team?

16. Who got the game-winning hit in Game 1 of the 2000 World Series vs. the New York Mets?

17. How many times has a Yankees pitcher won at least 25 games in a season?

18. Derek Jeter is the only player who had 3,000 hits in a Yankees uniform. Name the other seven who had 2,000 hits as a Yankee.

19. When the Yankees won their first American League pennant in 1921, in what stadium did they play their home games?

20. Name the 1962 movie that starred Yankees greats Mickey Mantle and Roger Maris. Bonus: Name the three other Yankees who appeared as themselves.

21. Who hit the last home run at Yankee Stadium I?

22. In the history of Yankee Stadium I, which pitcher had the best ERA?

23. When Yankee Stadium opened in 1923, what were the outfield dimensions?

24. There were four All-Star Games played at Yankee Stadium I. Name the two Yankees managers who piloted the American League team in two of those games.

25. Name the two Yankees rookies who had back-to-back home runs in their first major league at-bats.

26. Which Yankees pitcher hit an inside-the-park grand slam?

27. Which Yankees pitcher has the most wins in All-Star Game history?

28. On April 17, 1951, Mickey Mantle made his major league debut. Another notable figure in Yankees history also made his debut that day. Name him.

29. Who was the Yankees' first pick in baseball's first amateur draft in 1965?

30. Which Negro League great was rumored to have hit a ball completely out of Yankee Stadium in the 1930s?

31. Babe Ruth hit the first home run at Yankee Stadium I. Which player got the first Yankee hit?

32. On April 6, 1974, the Yankees played their first game at Shea Stadium. Yankee Stadium was being renovated and the team would play in Queens, New York, for the 1974 and 1975 seasons. The Yankees beat the Cleveland Indians, 6–1, in that opening game. Who was the first Yankees player who hit a home run in that game?

Bonus: Who scored the walkoff run in the Yankees' final game at Shea as the home team in 1975?

33. Name the pitcher who had a signature pitch called the "folly floater." Bonus: The same player was a two-sport athlete who played in the NBA. What pro basketball team did he play for?

34. Lou Gehrig began his record-setting streak of 2,130 games on June 1, 1925, when he entered the game as a pinch-hitter. Whom did he bat for?

35. Who was the only Yankees pitcher who batted as a designated hitter in the starting lineup? Bonus: Name the last Yankees pitcher to hit a home run before the DH rule was put into effect.

36. Name the free agent pitcher who signed a record contract with the Yankees on New Year's Eve in 1974.

37. Which Yankees pitcher lost three games in the 1981 World Series?

38. Who holds the franchise record for home runs by a rookie switch-hitter?

39. Which pitcher holds the franchise record for issuing the most walks in one game?

40. Which player became the first Yankee to hit a home run in his first major league at-bat?

ROOKIE-LEVEL ANSWERS

1. On June 22, 1962, the Yankees beat the Detroit Tigers at Tiger Stadium, 9–7, in a franchise record 22 innings. The game lasted exactly seven hours.

Backup outfielder Jack Reed had a moment in the sun as he hit a two-run homer in the top of the 22nd inning off Tigers reliever Phil Regan to give the Yankees the win. Reed spent all three seasons of his big league career with the Yankees, serving mostly as a defensive replacement in late innings for Mickey Mantle. A total of 43 players would be used in the game (21 for the Yankees, 22 for the Tigers). Each team used seven pitchers. Jim Bouton tossed shutout ball over the final seven innings to earn the win, while Regan took the loss.

The Tigers had the winning run on third with no one out in the bottom of the 11th and did not score. Rocky Colavito led off with a triple. After one out, Tigers catcher Dick Brown tried to squeeze the run home but bunted into a double play. In the top of the 22nd inning, Roger Maris walked with one out before Reed's home run snapped the tie. Bouton finished the game by retiring Norm Cash on a fly ball to left field with the tying run at the plate, as the clock hit seven hours.

2. When left-handed hitter Ron Blomberg stepped to the plate for the Yankees at Fenway Park, he officially became the first designated hitter in baseball history.

On January 11, 1973, the American League owners had voted 8–4 to institute the use of a "designated hitter" for a trial run of three years. In the first game of the season on April 6th, Blomberg was penciled in to bat sixth in the Yankees lineup. In the top of the first, the Yanks loaded the bases with two out and that gave the 24-year-old left-handed hitter an opportunity to etch his name into the record books as the first "D-H." Blomberg walked to force in a run; his bat was sent to the Baseball Hall of Fame in Cooperstown. The Atlanta, Georgia, native had been the number one overall selection by the Yankees in the 1967 amateur draft.

Blomberg, who is of Jewish heritage, idolized Mickey Mantle. In high school, he was given the moniker "the Jewish Mickey Mantle" for his power-hitting exploits. His left-handed swing was considered a perfect fit for the short right field porch in Yankee Stadium.

Injuries would plague Blomberg throughout his career. He retired after the 1978 season.

3. Second baseman Bobby Richardson caught a hard hit line drive off the bat of Willie McCovey to end the seventh and deciding game of the 1962 World Series against San Francisco.

The Yankees were leading the San Francisco Giants, 1–0, in the ninth inning of Game 7.

The Giants had runners on second and third with two out, and Hall of Famer Willie McCovey (who was one of the most feared hitters of that era) was the batter. Ralph Terry, who was victimized two years earlier by the Pirates' Bill Mazeroski for a walkoff home run in Game 7 of the 1960 World Series, was once again on the mound for the Yankees.

Hall of Famer Orlando Cepeda was on deck, but Yankees manager Ralph Houk and Terry decided to go after McCovey. The intimidating and powerful left-handed hitter smacked a hard line drive right at Richardson, who put his glove up and held on to the baseball to clinch the Series for the Yankees.

Richardson was one of the best second basemen in Yankee history. In 1960, the native of South Carolina became the only player to win the World Series Most Valuable Player Award while playing on the losing team. The 5'9" Richardson set a record with 12 runs batted in, including six in one game. He played in seven World Series and had a career average of .305 in the Fall Classic. Richardson spent his entire 12-year career with the Yankees and retired after the 1966 season.

4. On October 22, 1974, the Yankees traded popular out-fielder Bobby Murcer to the San Francisco Giants in exchange for two-time All-Star outfielder Bobby Bonds.

Murcer was signed as an 18-year-old in 1964 because the Yankees figured his left-hand bat could take advantage of the short right field porch at Yankee Stadium.

Murcer's best season was 1972, when he slammed 33 home runs and finished second in the American League with a .331 average.

From his first full season of 1969 through the 1973 season, Murcer hit a total of 129 home runs. When the Yankees moved to Shea Stadium in 1974, it became painfully obvious that the short right field dimensions at Yankee Stadium had helped enhance his power totals.

Murcer was traded from the Giants to the Chicago Cubs in 1977. He was dealt back to the Yankees on June 26, 1979. The tragic death of Yankees catcher and captain Thurman Munson led to Murcer's signature Yankee moment. Four days after Munson died, the entire team attended the funeral in Canton, Ohio. Murcer delivered the eulogy in honor of his close friend. That night, the Yankees hosted the Baltimore Orioles. Murcer paid tribute to his late friend by driving in all five runs, including a walkoff two-run single, in an emotional 5–4 Yankees win.

In 1975, Bobby Bonds became the first Yankee to record a "30–30" season. He hit 32 home runs and stole 30 bases in his only season with the Yankees.

5. Hall of Famer Joe McCarthy is the winningest manager in Yankees franchise history.

McCarthy won 1,460 games and had a .627 winning percentage during his 16 years with the team. As a result of his

Joe McCarthy's 1,460 wins is a franchise record for Yankees managers. Here he is before the 1937 All-Star Game with Bill Terry. (Library of Congress)

strict managerial style, he became known as "Marse Joe," short for "Master Joe."

McCarthy won eight American League pennants and seven World Series with the Yankees, including four in a row from 1936 to 1939.

Before coming to New York, McCarthy managed the Chicago Cubs for five seasons. He won 94 games in his first season with the Yankees, and finished second in the American League in 1931. The next season, he won his first American League pennant and World Series title as the Yankees swept his old team, the Cubs, in four games.

McCarthy and the Yankees would not return to the Series until 1936, when they began their run of four in a row. "Marse Joe"'s only World Series loss as Yankees manager came in 1942, when they lost to the St. Louis Cardinals in five games.

The Yankees met the Cardinals again in 1943, but this time New York prevailed in five games, giving McCarthy his seventh and final World Series championship in pinstripes. McCarthy retired after the 1946 season, but returned two years later to manage the Boston Red Sox for three seasons.

6. In December of 1992, the Yankees sent pitchers Russ Springer and Jerry Nielsen, along with first baseman J.T. Snow, to the California Angels in exchange for left-handed pitcher Jim Abbott. The young lefty was born with a deformed right arm, yet managed to become a major league pitcher. Abbott overcame his handicap by using a right-handed glove. He would engage the stub end of his deformed right arm to "carry" the glove, web down. After he finished his delivery, he would slide his left hand into the glove so that he was able to be in fielding position.

In 1993, Abbott would have an up and down first season in New York, but it all came together for a day on September 4th, when the amazing left-hander no-hit the Cleveland Indians at Yankee Stadium. Abbott had the excited crowd of 27,125 on their feet as he took the mound for the ninth with a 4–0 lead. After getting the first two outs, switch-hitter Carlos Baerga was the only obstacle standing in the way of a memorable game.

Abbott's slider was so good that day that Baerga batted left-handed against the Yankees' southpaw in his final at-bat. The Indians' second baseman hit a groundball to shortstop Randy Velarde, who fielded it and threw over to first baseman Don Mattingly for the final out.

Abbott would finish a disappointing 11–14 in 1993. In the strike-shortened season of 1994, the left-hander went 9–8 and would see his Yankees career end as he was allowed to become a free agent.

7. Harold "Butch" Wynegar caught Dave Righetti's no-hitter against the Boston Red Sox in 1983. In May of 1982, Wynegar was traded from the Minnesota Twins to the Yankees as part of a five-player deal. The 27-year-old, switch-hitting catcher played parts of five seasons with the Yankees.

In November of 1978, the Yankees dealt popular closer Sparky Lyle to the Texas Rangers to acquire promising young left-hander Dave Righetti as the centerpiece of a nine-player trade. The 20-year old southpaw began to live up to that promise when he won the American League Rookie of the Year Award in the strike-shortened 1981 season.

The 6'4" left-hander essentially had two Yankee careers. As a starter, "Rags" won 33 games from 1981 to 1983. After

Hall of Fame closer Rich "Goose" Gossage left as a free agent following the 1983 season, the Yankees moved Righetti to the bullpen, where he became the closer through the 1990 season.

July 4, 1983, would go down as the bookmark date of Righetti's 11-year tenure in New York. Boston featured a solid lineup headed by the American League's leading hitter, third baseman Wade Boggs. With the game time temperature at a steamy 94 degrees, the left-hander began the game with three strikeouts, sandwiched around a two-out walk, and rolled through the middle innings.

In the ninth, Righetti issued a leadoff walk. After the next two batters grounded out, only Boggs stood between Righetti and history. Boggs did not strike out much, but Righetti threw a 2–2 slider and the Red Sox third baseman swung and missed to end the gem.

8. In 1951, infielder Gil McDougald became the first Yankee to win the American League's Rookie of the Year Award. The Korean War had taken some players away from their teams while others were waiting to be called, including Yankees second baseman Jerry Coleman. In late April, McDougald got a start at third base and began to make the most of his opportunity. McDougald finished his rookie season with a .306 batting average, .396 on base percentage, 14 home runs, 63 runs batted in, and 72 runs scored.

The versatile Yankee played on three World Series–winning teams in his first three seasons, and won a total of five championships during his 10-year career with the Yankees. In 1955, McDougald was struck in the head by a line drive off the bat of teammate Bob Cerv during batting practice.

He was diagnosed with a concussion and came back a few days later. What went undetected was a skull fracture and damage to McDougald's left inner ear that diminished his hearing as he got older.

In 1957, McDougald was involved in an infamous incident that curtailed a pitcher's promising career. McDougald was the second batter in a game against Cleveland Indians hard-throwing left-hander Herb Score, and he lined a 2–2 pitch directly off the pitcher's right eye. The ball caromed to the third baseman, who threw McDougald out at first.

Score went to the hospital with numerous facial fractures. The incident upset McDougald to the extent that he couldn't sleep that night. The talented Indians southpaw would never be the same after that. He retired five years later at the age of 28. McDougald retired following the 1960 season.

9. Babe Ruth's numbers with the Yankees:

Stolen bases	110
Caught stealing	117
Triples	106
RBI	1,978
Walks	1,852
Strikeouts	1,122
Hit by pitch	35

Babe Ruth certainly did not look the part, but he amassed 110 stolen bases during his Yankee career. His most famous stolen base attempt occurred in the 1926 World Series. In the bottom of the ninth of Game 7, the Yankees were trailing the St Louis Cardinals, 3–2. With two out and no one on, Ruth walked to become the tying run, but he was thrown out trying

Babe Ruth slams one of three home runs during a doubleheader at the Polo Grounds in 1920. In the inset, a shirtless Ruth shows off his impressive wingspan. (Library of Congress)

to steal second to end the Series. Ruth was caught stealing 117 times as a Yankee.

While with the Yankees, Ruth played his home games at both the spacious Polo Grounds and Yankee Stadium, which featured the short right field porch designed to take advantage of his left-handed power. The left-center field gap was known as "Death Valley" because of its vast dimensions.

The dimensions of Ruth's home ballparks probably contributed more to his 106 triples than did his speed. Hitting 659 home runs would help produce a lot of runs batted in. Ruth had 1,978 RBIs as a Yankee, which accounted for 89 percent of his career total of 2,214. While wearing the pinstripes, Ruth drew 1,852 walks and struck out 1,122 times. Both numbers accounted for a significant percentage of his career totals (2,062 walks and 1,330 strikeouts). With the Yankees, Ruth was hit by a pitched ball 35 times. Remarkably, during his record-setting season of 1927, Ruth did not get hit once.

10. When a hitter records a single, double, triple, and home run in the same game, in baseball vernacular he "hits for the

Bob Meusel is the only player in franchise history to hit for the cycle three times. (Library of Congress)

cycle." Yankees outfielder Bob Meusel is the only player in franchise history to "hit for the cycle" three times in his career.

Meusel is one of only four players in all of baseball history who have ever reached the box score filling statistic that many times. The Los Angeles native was a terrific all around ballplayer who flew under the radar because he played with the Babe Ruth/Lou Gehrig Yankees in the 1920s. In May of 1921, Meusel hit for the cycle for the first time against Washington Senators Hall of Fame pitcher Walter Johnson. The second time occurred 14 months later when Meusel hit for the cycle and drove in six runs in a 12–1 win in Philadelphia against the Athletics.

On July 26th, in the first game of a doubleheader at Detroit's Navin Field against the Tigers, Meusel joined a select list of players. The game was tied at 1 through nine innings. Meusel's sixth-inning home run accounted for the Yankees' only run, and that was his only hit of the game going into the ninth when he doubled and was left stranded on base. In the 11th, Meusel singled and was a triple away from completing the statistical achievement. In the top of the 12th, Meusel got the three-base hit as part of a record-setting, extra-inning output of 11 runs, en route to a 12–1 win.

Meusel played 10 seasons with the Yankees.

11. On April 14, 1955, Elston Howard became the first black player in Yankees history when he made his major league debut at Boston's Fenway Park. Howard did not start, but he played left field and got his first major league hit and RBI in his first at-bat. It was an historic moment for the Yankees franchise.

After Jackie Robinson broke baseball's color barrier in 1947, other teams began following suit. Social change was taking place and the Yankees were being pressured to add a black player. The 6'2" Missouri native signed with the Yankees in 1950. In the 1955 World Series vs. the Brooklyn Dodgers, Howard hit a home run in his first at-bat. But he also made the final out in the Series, clinching the Game 7 defeat.

Howard played a large role in the 1958 World Series comeback vs. the Milwaukee Braves. In Game 5, Howard made a defensive play in left field that many felt turned the Series around. The Yankees trailed three games to one and had a 1–0 lead in the sixth. Milwaukee had a man on and no one out when second baseman Red Schoendienst lined a ball to left. Howard made a diving catch and then doubled off the runner at first.

In Game 7, Howard drove in the go-ahead run in the eighth and was named the World Series Most Valuable Player. In 1963, Howard became the first African-American to win the American League MVP.

In August of 1967, the Yankees traded the 38-year-old Howard to the Red Sox, where he helped Boston win their first pennant since 1946. The Yankees retired Howard's number 32 in 1984.

12. Rookie catcher Gary Sanchez became the fastest player in major league history to hit his first 11 home runs. In 2016, the 6'2" catcher hit an opposite field home run off Baltimore Orioles pitcher Dylan Bundy for his 11th home run in his 23rd major league game.

The Yankees signed the 16-year-old Dominican Republic native in 2009. Sanchez was physically gifted, and the Yankees were excited about his offensive potential. As the youngster worked his way through the Yankees' minor league system, the highly rated prospect was trying to clear some emotional hurdles. In 2014, the 21-year-old was suspended from the Yankees' AA affiliate at Trenton and was developing a reputation for a lack of work ethic. The young catcher was apparently more interested in his hitting than in his defense behind the plate. Sanchez was blessed with a strong arm, but not much else when it came to the nuances of the position.

In 2015, Sanchez started to develop as an all-around player. The catcher began the year at the Yankees' AA affiliate at Trenton, but was promoted to AAA Scranton Wilkes-Barre, where he played 35 games and drove in 26 runs. Sanchez competed for the backup catching job with the Yankees in spring training in 2016 but he began the year at AAA. In early August, the 23-year-old was brought up to the majors and went on his record-setting tear. He ended up hitting 20 home runs in his rookie season and finished second in the voting for the American League Rookie of the Year Award.

13. The Yankees have scored 20 or more runs in a game 29 times.

In July of 1920, the Yankees scored 20 runs for the first time in franchise history when they routed the Chicago White Sox, 20–5, at the Polo Grounds.

In May of 1936, the Yankees set a franchise record by pounding the Philadelphia Athletics, 25–2, at Philadelphia's Shibe Park. Second baseman Tony Lazzeri hit three home runs, including two grand slams, and drove in a record 11 runs.

The first time that the team scored 20 or more runs at Yankee Stadium was in the second game of a holiday doubleheader vs. the Washington Senators on July 4, 1927. The

Yankees, who won the opener, 12–1, used a nine-run outburst in the sixth inning to score a 21–1 win.

In May of 1930, Lou Gehrig drove in eight runs in a wild 20–13 win at Philadelphia's Shibe Park. The Yankees again beat the Athletics at Shibe Park in June of 1932, 20–13. Gehrig and Lazzeri combined for 12 runs batted in.

Mickey Mantle and Elston Howard combined for 15 RBIs in a 21–7 rout of the Kansas City Athletics in 1962 at Municipal Stadium in Kansas City.

In the 1931 and 1999 seasons, the Yankees scored 20 or more runs twice during the season.

In a 2005 game at Yankee Stadium vs. Tampa Bay, the Yankees nearly tied a franchise record (14) by scoring 13 runs in one inning as they went on to a 20–11 victory.

14. In their long and glorious history, Yankees pitchers have thrown 10 no-hitters in the regular season. Seven of those took place at Yankee Stadium. It wasn't until 1938 that a Yankee pitcher would toss a no-hit, no-run game at Yankee Stadium.

On August 27 of that year, 29-year-old Yankees right-hander Monte Pearson no-hit the Cleveland Indians in the second game of a doubleheader. It was the third no-hitter in franchise history.

Allie Reynolds's second no-hitter of 1951 was at the Stadium as the "Superchief" beat the Boston Red Sox. It took 32 years for another Yankees pitcher to throw a no-hitter at home. July 4, 1983, was owner George Steinbrenner's 53rd birthday and he couldn't have gotten a better birthday present, as young left-hander Dave Righetti no-hit the Boston Red Sox in a 4–0 win (see answer #7).

Left-hander Jim Abbott turned the trick when he no-hit the Cleveland Indians in 1993 (see answer #6).

In 1996, the Yankees began a stretch when they tossed three no-hitters in a four-year span.

Twelve years and one month after 19-year-old Dwight "Doc" Gooden made his much heralded major league debut for the New York Mets, the former Cy Young Award winner tossed a no-hitter for the Yankees against the Seattle Mariners.

In 1998 and 1999, the Yankees had perfect games tossed at the Stadium by David Wells and Cone, respectively (see MVP Level, question #1).

15. Before Babe Ruth joined the Yankees in 1920, they had never won a World Series.

In 1903, the franchise debuted as the New York Highlanders.

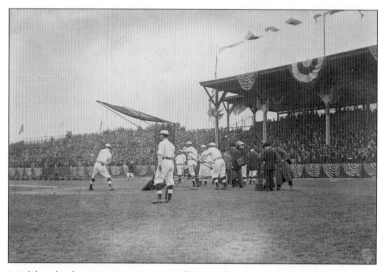

Highlander batting practice at Hilltop Park, 1911. (George Grantham Bain Collection, Library of Congress)

In their second season, the Highlanders finished a game and a half behind the pennant-winning Boston Americans in the American League. The Highlanders trailed the Americans by a half game with five games remaining against each other. New York won the first game, 3–2, to take a half-game lead in the American League, but the Americans swept a doubleheader the next day to take a game-and-a-half lead with two to play. On the final day of the season, the Americans won the opening game of a doubleheader, 3–2, to clinch the pennant.

In late July, John McGraw, the manager of the National League champion New York Giants, had pledged not to play the Highlanders if they won the American League. Fearful of losing to the AL champs, he followed through on his promise, and there was no World Series in 1904.

New York Giants manager John McGraw did not want to play the New York Highlanders, so there was no World Series played in 1904. (Library of Congress)

Two years later the Highlanders finished in second place, three games behind the pennant winning Chicago White Sox. The team finished second one more time, in 1910. In 1913, they became the New York Yankees and would not win the World Series until 1923.

16. Second baseman Jose Vizcaino ended Game 1 of the 2000 World Series with a walkoff RBI single in the bottom of the 12th inning. The City of New York was experiencing its first "Subway Series" since 1956, when the Yankees played the Brooklyn Dodgers. The opening game at Yankee Stadium was scoreless with two out in the top of the sixth when the Yankees made a memorable defensive play. Mets right fielder Timo Perez was on first when Todd Zeile hit a ball that bounded off of the left field wall. Perez, thinking the ball was going to be a home run, let up on the bases and was eventually thrown out at home thanks to a great relay throw from Yankees shortstop Derek Jeter.

The Yankees trailed 3–2 in the ninth, but rallied to tie the game and send it into extra innings. With two out and the bases loaded in the 12th inning, Vizcaino lined a single towards the left field line to score Tino Martinez with the game-winning run in a 4–3 Yankees win.

Vizcaino had his only four hits of the entire Series in Game 1. The Yankees had acquired Vizcaino in June from the Los Angeles Dodgers in exchange for catcher Jim Leyritz. Vizcaino played in 73 games as a Yankee and hit .276.

17. Five Yankees pitchers won 25 or more games in a season. One did it twice. (Note: Jack Chesbro won 41 games for the New York Highlanders in 1904.)

In 1920, right-handed pitcher Carl Mays set a Yankees franchise record of 26 wins, only to break it the next season with a league-leading 27 victories.

It wasn't as heralded as the 1919 trade with the Boston Red Sox that brought Babe Ruth to the Yankees, but nearly two years after that historic deal the Yankees made another trade with their neighbors to the northeast. As part of a seven-player trade with the Bosox, the Yankees acquired pitcher Joe Bush. In 1922, his first year with the Yankees, Bush finished second in the American League with 26 wins.

Hall of Famer Lefty Gomez spent parts of 13 seasons with the Yankees, but his best season was 1934, when he posted 26 wins to go along with a 2.33 ERA and 25 complete games.

Joe Bush won 26 games in 1922, his first year with the Yankees. (Library of Congress)

Hall of Famer Edward "Whitey" Ford put together a spectacular 16-year career in Yankees pinstripes. His best season was 1961, when he won 25 games and was named the American League Cy Young Award winner.

In 1977, a 27-year-old left-hander named Ron Guidry blossomed into a 16-game winner. He did a lot better in 1978. The Louisiana native put together what is arguably the greatest single season of pitching in franchise history . Guidry posted a sparkling 25–3 record with a league leading 1.74 ERA.

18. Derek Jeter is the only player to amass 3,000 hits as a Yankee. He finished his career with 3,465. The seven other Yankees to have 2,000 hits include:

- Lou Gehrig   2,721
- Babe Ruth   2,518
- Mickey Mantle   2,415
- Bernie Williams   2,336
- Joe DiMaggio   2,215
- Don Mattingly   2,153
- Yogi Berra   2,148

Of that list, Ruth and Berra are the only two to have played with another team besides the Yankees. Ruth played with the Boston Red Sox before coming to the Yankees, and with the Boston Braves afterwards. Berra played in parts of three seasons with the New York Mets.

Gehrig, DiMaggio, Mantle, Mattingly, and Jeter all singled for their final Yankees hits.

Ruth and Berra homered, while Bernie Williams's final Yankee hit was a pinch-hit double.

Jeter's 3,000th hit was a home run off Tampa Bay Rays pitcher David Price in 2011.

Derek Jeter watches his 3,000th hit, a home run off the Rays' David Price, sail toward the seats on July 9, 2011. (AP Photo/Bill Kostroun)

19. In 1921, the Yankees played their home games at the Polo Grounds in upper Manhattan. The Yankees shared the ballpark with the New York Giants from 1913 to 1922.

In February of 1921, the team announced the purchase of 10 acres of land in the West Bronx that would eventually become the site of Yankee Stadium.

In 1921, Carl Mays became the Yanks' first pitcher to win a World Series game. (Library of Congress)

The Yankees won their first American League pennant in 1921, while their co-tenants won their eighth National League pennant. The Giants and Yankees already had made some news together (see: answer #15).

1921 was the final year that the Series was a best-of-nine competition. Yankees right hander Carl Mays tossed a complete game, five-hit shutout in a 3–0, Game 1 victory.

The Yankees were the road team in Game 1, but the teams alternated home and road throughout the Series (unlike today's schedule, which calls for Games 1, 2, 6 and 7 to be played at one venue, with Games 3, 4 and 5 at the other site).

The Yanks took Game 2 by the same score, but their rivals won the next two. The Giants won Game 7, and then took the Series in Game 8 with a 1–0 win.

In 1922, the teams met again. This time, it was a best-of-seven Series. The Giants scored a four-game sweep, but it was really a five-game Series as Game 2 finished in a tie due to darkness and was replayed.

20. In 1962, Yankees greats Mickey Mantle and Roger Maris starred in a movie entitled *Safe at Home.*

The film centers on a young boy who tells a lie that his father knows Mantle and Maris, and promises to bring them to his Little League's team banquet. Ten-year-old Hutch Lawton (played by child actor Bryan Russell, who was also in the movie *Bye Bye Birdie*) recently moved from New York to Florida with Ken Lawton, his widowed dad. In the film, Mr. Lawton runs a charter fishing boat and doesn't have time to attend Hutch's Little League games. After one of Hutch's obnoxious teammates teases him that his dad doesn't come to the games because he doesn't know baseball, Hutch brags that his father is good friends with Mantle and Maris. One of the coaches overhears the conversation, and that prompts Hutch to brag that the two Yankees stars would attend their Little League banquet.

In order to avoid having to tell the truth, Hutch goes to the Yankees' spring training site in Fort Lauderdale to try and recruit the two players. He sneaks into the clubhouse and meets the Yankee stars, and a Yankee coach (played by William Frawley, who was Fred Mertz in TV's *I Love Lucy*). Hutch tells his story, but at first they turn down his request.

When Hutch returns home to confess that he wasn't truthful, he learns that Mantle and Maris have saved his reputation by inviting his entire Little League team to join them at spring training.

The two Yankees stars are far from being polished actors, but they're not in the movie for their acting abilities.

Other Yankees who appeared in the movie as themselves include Manager Ralph Houk, pitcher Whitey Ford, and first baseman Joe Pepitone.

21. Yankee catcher Jose Molina hit the last home run at Yankee Stadium I.

That Stadium opened in 1923 and was remodeled during the 1974–75 seasons.

In 2006, the Yankees broke ground for a new Yankee Stadium that would be built across the street from the site of the original Stadium. On September 21, 2008, the Yankees hosted the Baltimore Orioles in the final game at the older structure that was affectionately referred to as "the cathedral of baseball." For a lavish pre-game ceremony on that final day, the Yankees brought back many of their all-time greats from the past. In that game, in the bottom of the fourth, Molina hit a two-run home run over the left-center field wall. With that final game came a list of "lasts."

Andy Pettitte was the last winning pitcher at the original Yankee Stadium; Mariano Rivera retired Orioles second baseman Brian Roberts on a groundout to first baseman Cody Ransom for the final out, and Derek Jeter was the last Yankee batter. In the bottom of the eighth, Jeter grounded out to third. Jason Giambi singled in the seventh for the last Yankees hit in the old ballpark, and Brett Gardner scored the final run.

From 1923 to 2008 (minus the 1974 and 1975 seasons at Shea), the Yankees posted a record of 4,133 wins, 2,430 losses and 17 ties . . . a solid 63 percent winning percentage in front of home fans.

22. The franchise leader in career ERA at the original Yankee Stadium is left-hander Fritz Peterson.

The southpaw started 167 games at the Stadium and posted a 2.52 ERA. Peterson began his nine-year Yankee career in 1966. He made the team out of spring training and was inserted in the starting rotation. The 24-year-old tossed 215 innings and went 12–11 for a Yankees team that finished in last place—a rarity for this franchise. Peterson's best season was 1970, when he won 20 games and was named an American League All-Star.

Unfortunately for the Yankees left-hander, his most notable moment took place off the field. In March of 1973, Fritz Peterson stunned the baseball world with a story that transcended the sport. Peterson announced that he and his teammate, pitcher Mike Kekich, were trading their wives. The news set off a firestorm of controversy during spring training and seemed to affect Peterson on the field.

The southpaw did not pitch well in 1973 and finished with an 8–15 record. In April of 1974, Peterson was traded to the Cleveland Indians as part of a seven-player swap that became an historic footnote in Yankees history. As part of that deal, the Yankees got back first baseman Chris Chambliss and relief pitcher Dick Tidrow. Those two players would go on to play significant roles when the Yankees won back-to-back World Series titles in 1977 and 1978.

23. When Yankee Stadium opened in 1923, the center field wall was 490 feet from home plate.

It stayed that way through the 1927 season. Beginning with the 1928 season and lasting through 1936, the center field wall was 475 feet from home plate.

From 1923 to 1927, the left field foul pole measured 281 feet from home plate and was increased to 301 feet beginning in 1928.

Opening Day Ceremonies at Yankee Stadium, 1925. (Library of Congress)

Left-center field, or "Death Valley" as it came to be known, was 460 feet from 1923 to 1936. That area of the field got its nickname because it was so difficult to hit a ball that far in order to clear the fence. Beginning with the 1937 season Death Valley was barely shortened by a step to 457 feet, while it was 407 feet to the gap in right-center, and right field was 344 feet from home plate. It was 461 feet to dead center. From 1967 to 1973, the distance in center field was moved back to 463 feet.

In the "House That Ruth Built," the distance down the right field line ("the porch") was a mere 295 feet from 1923 to 1938. It was increased by one foot for the remainder of the original Stadium's tenure.

When the Stadium re-opened in 1976, the dimensions from left field to right field were:

Left field line—312 feet
Left field—387 feet
Left-center field—430 feet (aka "Death Valley")
Center field—417 feet
Right-center field—385 feet
Right field—353 feet
Right field line—310 feet

24. The original Yankee Stadium played host to four All-Star Games.

In two of those games, the Yankees manager piloted the American League team.

The first time was in 1939, when Joe McCarthy was the American League skipper. The second was in 1977, when Billy Martin ran the AL team.

On July 11, 1939, Yankee Stadium hosted its first All-Star Game. The starting lineup for the American League featured six Yankees, including the game's starting pitcher, Red Ruffing. A week after the Yankees retired his number 4, Lou Gehrig was named to the team as an honorary captain. The Yankee representatives accounted for three of the American League's six hits, including Joe DiMaggio's solo home run in the fifth that completed the scoring in a 3–1 win.

On July 19, 1977, the remodeled Yankee Stadium played host to the "Midsummer Classic" for a third time. The Yankees had been the 1976 American League pennant winners, so Yankees manager Billy Martin ran the AL squad. Second baseman Willie Randolph and outfielder Reggie Jackson were the only Yankees in the starting lineup. Closer Sparky Lyle, catcher Thurman Munson, and third baseman Graig Nettles were the other Yankees who made the team. The National League scored four runs in the top of the first and never looked back, as they went on to a 7–5 win.

25. Less than 24 hours after Alex Rodriguez's farewell in 2016, an infusion of new blood made memorable debuts.

Yankee rookies Tyler Austin and Aaron Judge gave the team's fans something to remember, slamming back-to-back home runs in their first major league at-bats. Austin and Judge were promoted from the minors as part of the youth movement that developed when the Yankees decided to trade away some of their older assets at midseason.

On August 13th, the Yankees hosted the Tampa Bay Rays. Austin and Judge were in the starting lineup hitting seventh and eighth, respectively, in the batting order. In the bottom of the second, Austin came up against Rays pitcher Matt Andriese and hit a ball toward the short right field porch that just reached the stands for his first big-league home run. Judge was next and he did one better. On a 1–2 pitch, the 6'7" slugger hit a prodigious blast that hit the "batter's eye glass" in dead center field at Yankee Stadium II.

It marked only the third time since the new Stadium had opened in 2009 that a batter reached that distance. The back-to-back feat marked the first time in baseball history that a pair of teammates hit home runs in the first at-bats of their major league debuts in the same game.

26. On July 20, 1965, Yankee pitcher Mel Stottlemyre hit an inside-the-park grand slam home run.

It was the fourth grand slam by a Yankees pitcher. The Yankees led the Boston Red Sox, 2–1, and had the bases loaded with no one out in the fifth. Stottlemyre, who was a very good hitting pitcher, clubbed the first pitch from Red Sox pitcher Bill Monbouquette into the spacious left-center field gap at the Stadium. Red Sox left fielder Carl Yastrzemski ran it down and fired the relay to shortstop Rico Petrocelli, but Stottlemyre was going all the way and he just beat the throw home. Stottlemyre debuted with the Yankees in August of 1964, when the team was locked in a tight pennant race. The right-hander won nine games down the stretch to help the Yankees win the pennant. In the World Series against the St. Louis Cardinals, Stottlemyre tossed a complete game victory in Game 2 to even the Series at a game apiece. He went toe to toe with Hall of Famer Bob Gibson for seven innings in Game 5, but the Yankees lost in extra innings. Both pitchers came back in Game 7, when Gibson outlasted the young Yankee hurler. The native of the state of Washington was one of the bright spots in an era during which the Yankees were not winning championships. Stottlemyre won 20 games in 1965, 1968, and 1969. After that, his numbers began to drop off. The right-hander suffered a rotator cuff injury that cut short his career, and he retired in August of 1974. Stottlemyre became the pitching coach for the Yankees' championship teams of the late 1990s.

27. Hall of Fame pitcher Lefty Gomez is the franchise leader with three All-Star wins.

Gomez started five of the first six All-Star Games, including the first one in 1933 at Chicago's Comiskey Park. He was not only the first winning pitcher; he also drove in the first ever run in an All-Star Game with a single in the second inning. The left-hander from Rodeo, California, started the 1934 game but did not get a decision, as the American League outlasted the National League, 9–7, at New York's Polo Grounds.

Gomez was the American League starter for the third straight year in 1935. The game was played at Cleveland Stadium. The Yankee left-hander pitched six innings to get his second All-Star win. Gomez made the team in 1936 but did not appear in the game. In 1937, Gomez made his fourth All-Star start and got his third win, as the American League topped the National League at Griffith Stadium in Washington, D.C. The Yankee left-hander made his final All-Star start and suffered his first loss in 1938. Gomez was victimized by an error filled contest, yielding one unearned run in a 4–1 National League win.

Gomez made his final All-Star team in 1939, but did not appear in the game at Yankee Stadium.

28. On the same day that Mickey Mantle made his major league debut, legendary public address announcer Bob Sheppard worked his first game.

The Yankees opened the 1951 season at Yankee Stadium on April 17. Mantle was batting third and playing right field. Sheppard introduced the starting lineups for the first time, and would continue to do so until 2007. After World War II, the Queens, New York–born Sheppard worked as a public address announcer for St. John University's football and basketball games. He was actually offered the Yankees job in 1948, but did not accept it until three years later. The microphone made his baritone voice and eloquent pronunciation sound stentorian.

Hall of Famer and former Yankee Reggie Jackson once referred to Sheppard as "the voice of God." That was after Sheppard introduced Jackson in a surprise appearance at Fenway Park when the Yankees played there. Sheppard not only worked Yankee games, he was the "in-house voice" for his beloved New York Giants, and continued to work when the proud NFL franchise moved to New Jersey in the mid-1970s.

Sheppard was at the P.A. mic when the Giants hosted the Baltimore Colts in the 1958 NFL Championship game, one that many call "the greatest game ever played."

The longtime P.A. announcer worked 4,500 baseball games for the Yankees—or "The Bronx Bombers," as they have often been called—including 22 World Series and six no-hitters, three of them perfect games. It was rare when Sheppard made a mistake but one did occur during a game in 1982. Yankees reliever Shane Rawley entered the game and promptly gave up the lead. Sheppard inadvertently left his microphone open and said "You call that relief pitching?" After the game, the proud and dignified man went to the locker room to apologize to Rawley. Sheppard died at the age of 99 in 2010.

29. In order to establish a competitive balance within the sport, Major League Baseball instituted an amateur draft in 1965.

A highly touted outfielder from Arizona State named Rick Monday was selected first overall by the Kansas City Athletics. The Yankees had the 19th overall pick; they chose a 6'4" right-handed pitcher out of Wahlert Hight School in Dickeyville, Wisconsin, named Bill Burbach. Burbach spent parts of three seasons with the Yankees, but he never thrived in the major leagues. The right-hander debuted in 1969, and in his second major league game he pitched a complete game, five-hit shutout against the Detroit Tigers in the second game of a doubleheader at Yankee Stadium. Burbach finished his first year with a 6–8 record, but he did not win a game after July 12th.

Over the next two seasons, Burbach would appear in six more games with the Yankees before being traded to the Baltimore Orioles for right-handed pitcher Jim Hardin in May of 1971.

30. In the early 20th century, African-American baseball players who were not being allowed to play major league baseball began to form their own teams.

The result of this movement was born in 1920, with the formation of the Negro National League. In the 1930s and 1940s, Yankee Stadium hosted Negro League baseball. Slugging catcher Josh Gibson was considered by many to be the greatest power hitter in the history of Negro League baseball. Gibson, who was called by some the "black Babe Ruth," was reported to have hit a ball completely out of Yankee Stadium during a Negro League game. No player had ever achieved this prodigious feat, but, like the legend of Ruth pointing to center field and then hitting the ball to that spot at Chicago's Wrigley

Field in the 1932 World Series, Gibson's home run has never been confirmed but continues to grow in legendary status.

Gibson's Homestead Grays team was playing the New York Lincoln Giants at Yankee Stadium. In the ninth, Gibson reportedly launched a mammoth home run off Giants pitcher Connie Rector that cleared the left field fence and the bullpen.

According to the book *Great Hitters of the Negro Leagues* by Paul Hoblin, Giants third baseman Bill Holland said, "the ball finally came down at the back of the bullpen."

Giants catcher Larry Brown said, "the ball bounced off the top of the back wall," but Grays manager William Johnson insisted that it did leave the Stadium.

In 1967, *The Sporting News* credited Gibson with hitting a 580-foot home run at Yankee Stadium that struck two feet from the top wall that circled the center field bleachers.

Josh Gibson's plaque at the Baseball Hall of Fame in Cooperstown, New York. (Delaywaves via Wikimedia Commons)

31. When Yankee Stadium opened for business on April 18, 1923, second baseman Aaron Ward was the first Yankee to get a hit in the new ballpark.

The actual first hit by either team was a second-inning single by Boston Red Sox first baseman (not the famous comedian) George Burns. Ward singled in the bottom half of the third for the first-ever Yankees hit, but he was thrown out at third for the second out of the inning. Later that inning, Babe Ruth hit the first home run. Ward joined the Yankees in August of 1917 but wasn't in the everyday lineup until 1920, when he became the starting third baseman. The incumbent, Frank "Home Run" Baker, sat out the season to care for his children after his wife's untimely death. When Baker returned in 1921, Yankees manager Miller Huggins moved Ward to second base, where he started for the next five seasons.

In the 1921 World Series, Ward, who was known as an outstanding fielder, was criticized for making a key error that allowed the Giants to win Game 7, 2–1, and take a four games to three lead in what was a best-of-nine Series at the time. The Yankees went on to lose in the eighth game.

Ward batted .417 in the 1923 World Series, and had a hit in each of the six games, as the Yankees won their first-ever world championship.

32. With Yankee Stadium going through a massive renovation in 1974 and 1975, the Yankees worked out an agreement with the New York Mets to play their home games at Shea Stadium during that time.

On April 6, 1974, the Yankees hosted the Cleveland Indians in their first home game in Queens. In the bottom of the fourth, third baseman Graig Nettles became the first

Yankee to homer at Shea. Nettles broke up a scoreless tie when he connected for a two-run shot off Indians pitcher and Hall of Famer Gaylord Perry. A crowd of a little fewer than 21,000 was on hand to see the Yankees beat Cleveland, 6–1. Bill Sudakis was the Yanks' first designated hitter at Shea, while Mel Stottlemyre tossed a complete game to become the Yanks' first winning pitcher in that stadium.

Perry had a reputation for throwing a spitball. A pitcher would apply a foreign substance onto the ball to give it movement and make it more effective against the hitters. This game marked the first time that Perry was called on it. Home plate umpire Marty Springstead issued a warning to Perry in the sixth inning for allegedly throwing a spitball.

The Yankees hosted the Baltimore Orioles in their final home game at Shea in 1975. The game ended when the winning run scored on a throwing error in the bottom of the ninth. Orioles pitcher Dyar Miller tried a pickoff play at third, but the throw went past third baseman Doug DeCinces, allowing Yankees catcher Rick Dempsey to score the final run of their Shea Stadium tenure.

33. Steve Hamilton was a tall left-handed reliever who threw a signature pitch called the "folly floater."

The folly floater is also known as an "eephus pitch." It's thrown overhand but comes in like a slow softball pitch with a high arcing trajectory. Hamilton began using the pitch later in his career. At 6'6", Hamilton would go into his windup and suddenly appear to stop short. He would then release the ball, which would tantalize the hitter as it approached the plate. The most famous time Hamilton used the pitch was in July of 1970 at Yankee Stadium against Cleveland. He was brought in to pitch the top of the ninth with the Yankees trailing, 7–2. Hamilton unleashed the folly floater and Indians first baseman Tony Horton took a big swing, but fouled it off to the delight of almost everyone in the ballpark, including his Indians teammates. Horton wanted that pitch again and Hamilton obliged. The right-handed hitter took another big swing and fouled it back toward the backstop behind home plate. Yankees catcher Thurman Munson took off after the ball and made a terrific one-handed catch to retire Horton. After the out, Cleveland's first baseman took a slow walk back to the dugout. A few feet before he arrived at the dugout steps, Horton crawled on all fours the rest of the way. Hamilton was a two-sport star who played for the NBA's Minneapolis Lakers during the 1958–59 season. He is one of two people (Gene Conley—1957 Milwaukee Braves, 1959–1961 Boston Celtics) to have played in both a World Series and an NBA Finals.

34. On June 1, 1925, Lou Gehrig began his record streak of 2,130 consecutive games played when he entered as a pinch-hitter.

Gehrig was batting for Yankee shortstop Pee-Wee Wanninger; he did not get a hit but the streak had begun. The next day, Yankees first baseman Wally Pipp was sidelined due to a concussion and the "Iron Horse" took his spot at first, where he stayed until 1939. Ironically, Wanninger replaced shortstop Everett Scott, who had the previous record of consecutive games played with 1,307. Scott's streak ended on May 5, 1925. Wanninger started at shortstop the next day, and was 0-for-2 before being removed for a pinch-hitter in the seventh inning.

It was thought that Scott would be used to bat for Wanninger to keep his streak alive, but Yankees manager Miller

Paul "Pee-Wee" Wanninger was known as the batter whom Lou Gehrig pinch-hit for to begin his record streak of 2,130 games. (Library of Congress)

Huggins sent up Ernie Johnson. Scott was reported to have "lame knees" as the reason for not being used in the game, but a conflicting report stated he was angry and had quit the team.

Wanninger started 110 games in 1925 (his only season with the Yankees). He batted .236 with a home run and 23 runs batted in. In December, the Yankees traded the 5'7" shortstop to St. Paul of the American Association as the player to be named later in a deal for catcher Pat Collins.

35. During his major league career, Rick Rhoden was known as a very good hitting pitcher.

With that in mind, manager Billy Martin started Rhoden as the designated hitter on June 11, 1988, when the Yankees hosted the Baltimore Orioles at Yankee Stadium. The team was plagued by injuries, so Martin felt the right-handed-hitting Rhoden was a better option against Baltimore Orioles southpaw Greg Ballard. After a groundout in his first at-bat, Rhoden's second at-bat was a bit more productive; he drove in a run with a sacrifice fly. Rhoden was lifted for a pinch-hitter in the fifth inning.

The Yankees acquired Rhoden as part of a six-player trade with the Pittsburgh Pirates, following the 1986 season. The Yankees viewed Rhoden as an ace. He posted a 16–10 record with a 3.86 ERA in his first season with the Yankees. In 1988, Rhoden dropped to 12–12 with a 4.29 ERA. In January of 1989, the Yankees traded Rhoden to the Houston Astros.

Since the implementation of the designated hitter rule in 1973, no Yankees pitcher has hit a home run, not even in interleague play. The last Yankees pitcher to hit a home run was Lindy McDaniel, who accomplished the feat in 1972. In late September, the Yankees were playing the Tigers in Detroit. McDaniel snapped a 1–1 tie with a solo home run in the ninth inning off Tigers lefty Mickey Lolich.

36. When free agency in baseball became a reality in the 1970s, Yankees owner George Steinbrenner knew full well how to take advantage of this new-found ability to bring in star players without having to give up any in a trade.

On New Year's Eve, 1974, the Yankees signed free agent pitcher Catfish Hunter to a record-setting five-year contract for $3.35 million. At the time, it made the All-Star pitcher the highest-paid player in the game.

Hunter had led the Oakland Athletics to their third straight world championship in the previous season. The right-hander from North Carolina won 25 games and led the American League with a 2.49 ERA. Thanks to a technicality in his contract with the Athletics, Hunter became a free agent after the season. In his first year with the Yankees, the Hall of Famer started off slowly by losing his first three decisions, but he rebounded to win 23 games. He also threw a league-leading 328 innings and tossed 30 complete games.

The North Carolina native helped the Yankees win back-to-back championships in 1977 and 1978. When the Yankees were making their epic comeback against the Boston Red Sox in 1978, Hunter overcame some arm issues to win nine of his last 11 decisions in August and September. Hunter retired following the 1979 season and was elected to the Baseball Hall of Fame in 1987.

37. Yankees relief pitcher George Frazier was the losing pitcher in three games of the 1981 World Series against the Los Angeles Dodgers.

The Oklahoma City native made his first appearance in Game 3 in Los Angeles. Frazier pitched two innings and gave up two runs as he took the first of his three losses. Yankees manager Bob Lemon went to Frazier in a key spot in Game 4. The game was tied at six in the seventh when the Yankees reliever put the go-ahead run on base. After that run eventually scored, Frazier absorbed his second straight loss as the Dodgers evened up the

Series at two games apiece. The Dodgers won Game 5 and the Yankees were facing elimination in Game 6 at Yankee Stadium. With the game tied at 1 in the fifth, Frazier gave up three runs. The Dodgers won the game and the Series as the Yankees' reliever tied a record with three losses in a single World Series.

That record had been set by Chicago White Sox pitcher "Lefty" Williams in the scandal-scarred 1919 World Series. Williams was suspected of being involved with the infamous "Black Sox" scandal in which some White Sox players purposely lost games and the Series.

Frazier pitched two more seasons for the Yankees before being traded to the Cleveland Indians before the 1984 season.

38. In 1962, switch-hitting rookie Tom Tresh walloped 20 home runs to set a franchise record.

Going into the 1962 season, the Yankees needed a shortstop. The incumbent, Tony Kubek, was called to duty with the National Guard and was expected to miss most of the season. Yankees manager Ralph Houk liked the fact that Tresh was a switch-hitter, so he penciled in the 23-year-old to man the position. When Kubek returned in August Houk moved Tresh to left field, where he would eventually become a Gold Glove winner. The Detroit native was an All-Star in his first year, playing in 157 games and hitting .286 with 93 RBIs.

Tresh carried his outstanding first season into the World Series against the San Francisco Giants. The first year switch-hitter batted .321, with five runs scored in the seven-game victory. Tresh made a key defensive play in the seventh and deciding game. The Yankees had a 1–0 lead with one out and no one on in the bottom of the seventh. Willie Mays came up and hit a line drive that seemed headed for the left field corner.

Tresh raced over towards the foul line and made a spectacular, backhanded catch to rob Mays of what would have been a sure double. That play proved to be a big one as the Yankees held on for a 1–0 Series-clinching win.

Tresh was named the 1962 American League Rookie of the Year, becoming the third Yankee to win the award.

39. Yankees left-hander Tommy Byrne holds the franchise record by walking 13 batters in a single game.

The infamous achievement took place at Detroit's Briggs Stadium on June 8, 1949. Byrne went the distance in an 11-inning, 3–2 loss that ended when Tigers right fielder Vic Wertz singled with the bases loaded. Byrne loaded the bases with his final three walks before yielding the walkoff hit. The Tigers let the Wake Forest graduate off the hook by leaving 14 men on base.

In the first inning Byrne walked the first two hitters, but gave up only one run thanks to a base-running mistake by Detroit that led to a doubleplay. Two walks from Byrne to begin the second led to Detroit's second run. The Yankees' southpaw scattered the walks until it finally caught up to him in the 11th inning.

Byrne had two separate stints with the Yankees. From 1943 to 1951 (with two years removed for military service), Byrne won 42 of his 72 wins with the Yankees. The team traded Byrne to the St. Louis Browns in June of 1951, but he was brought back in 1954.

Byrne's best season was 1955, when he was 16–5 with a 3.15 ERA for the American League champs.

40. In 1966, outfielder John Miller became the first Yankee to hit a home run in his first major league at-bat.

Miller played a total of six games for the Yankees, but he had that memorable moment in his first game on September 11th. The Yankees were playing the Boston Red Sox at Fenway Park. Miller started in left field and was batting seventh. In the top of the second, Miller hit a two-run homer off Red Sox right hander Lee Stange in his first at-bat in the big leagues. The Yankees won the game, 4–2, in 10 innings.

Miller started five more games for the remainder of the 1966 season, but did not get another hit in a Yankees uniform. Miller's career slash line with the Yankees: .087/.087/.304.

In April of 1967, the Yankees traded Miller to the Los Angeles Dodgers in exchange for utility infielder John Kennedy.

2

ALL-STAR LEVEL

(Answers begin on page 55.)

You've successfully navigated your way through the first chapter; now you're ready to take the next step.

This chapter gets a little more difficult as we continue to focus on great names, great games, and memorable moments with great questions. See if you can come up with the correct answers.

1. Name the Yankee outfielder who was nicknamed "Old Reliable."

2. Who was the last Yankees pitcher to toss a complete game postseason win?

3. In Game 1 of the 1997 American League Championship Series vs. Cleveland, three Yankees hit back-to-back-to-back home runs in the sixth inning. Name those three players.

4. Name the former Yankees pitcher who wrote a revealing "tell-all" in 1970 about what went on behind the scenes of a baseball team.

5. Name the three Yankees who hit grand slams in the same game to set a major league record. Bonus: In that game, what position did Jorge Posada play for the only time in a major league game?

6. Name the Yankee who made a game-saving catch in the seventh game of the 1952 World Series.

7. He was known as "Super Chief," and he's the only Yankees pitcher to throw two no-hitters in the same season. Name him.

8. How many Yankees managers also played for the team?

9. In Games 4 and 5 of the 2001 World Series, the Yankees twice tied the game on two-run home runs in the bottom of the ninth. Who were those two players who hit the home runs?

10. In the 2001 postseason, Derek Jeter hit a walkoff home run to win Game 4 of the World Series. Name the other Yankee to hit a postseason walkoff home run in 2001.

11. In early September of 1964, the Yankees made a late season move to acquire a reliever from the Cleveland Indians to enhance their chances of winning the American League pennant. This right-hander went on to record eight saves down the stretch. Name him.

12. Who am I? I was known for being a two-sport athlete. The Yankees chose me in the 30th round of the 1988 amateur draft out of Florida State. I hit an inside-the-park home run and scored an NFL touchdown.

13. In 1998, the Yankees' designated hitter Darryl Strawberry tied a major league record as a pinch-hitter. What was that record?

14. In December of 1975, which two players did the Yankees receive from the California Angels in exchange for outfielder Bobby Bonds?

15. Who holds the franchise record for most stolen bases in World Series play?

16. Name the eight Yankees who hit World Series grand slams.

17. This Yankees pitcher became the first reliever to win the American League Cy Young Award. Bonus: Name the pitcher the Yankees got back when they traded the player who is the answer to this question to Texas in 1978.

18. In 1975, the Yankees and Minnesota Twins played to a 6–6 tie after 14 innings at Shea Stadium. The game was suspended and later completed in Minnesota. The Yankees were the home team at Minneapolis's Metropolitan Stadium and won the completion of the suspended game in 16 innings. Who was the player who had the walkoff hit in that game?

19. Do you know how many games make up the longest winning streak in franchise history?

20. In the seventh game of the 1960 World Series, a Yankees shortstop was hit in the adam's apple by a bad hop single. Many observers felt that incident turned the game. Who was that shortstop? Bonus: Name the batter who hit that ball, and would later go on to manage the Yankees.

21. Who is the only Yankee who has hit two home runs in one inning twice?

22. Derek Jeter had three hits in a single All-Star Game. In fact, he did it twice. Who is the only other Yankee to have three hits in an All-Star Game?

23. Lou Gehrig's number 4 was the first number ever retired by the Yankees. Babe Ruth's number 3 was second. Casey Stengel's number 37 was the _____ (numerical order) ever retired by the Yankees.

24. On September 30, 1973, the Yankees lost, 8–5, to the Detroit Tigers in the final game ever played at the original Yankee Stadium. _____ hit the final Yankee home run. Bonus: Name the Yankee who got the last hit and the player who made the last out.

25. In 1998, the Yankees played one home game at Shea Stadium because of a structural problem at Yankee Stadium. The Bombers beat the Anaheim Angels, 6–3. Which Yankee hit a home run in that game and why was it significant? Bonus: Who got the save?

26. Which other Yankee, besides Bucky Dent, homered for the Yankees in the one-game playoff vs. Boston in 1978?

27. Name the two players who were involved in a famous locker room brawl in 1979?

28. Who am I? In the 1960s I was a defensive stalwart at third base, yet never won a Gold Glove as a Yankee. I played against my brother in the World Series. I was traded to Atlanta and replaced a Hall of Famer.

29. Name the two position players who pitched for the Yankees on back-to-back days in the 1968 season.

30. Mariano Rivera was the last Yankee to wear uniform number 42. Who was the first?

ALL-STAR LEVEL ANSWERS

1. Tommy Henrich earned his nickname, "Old Reliable," for his uncanny ability to hit in the clutch.

The Massillon, Ohio, native was signed by the Cleveland Indians in 1934. He played for the Indians for three years in the minors before being released in April of 1937. Henrich, who was not big in stature (6', 180 pounds) put up some impressive numbers during his minor league stint in the Indians organization, but he felt Cleveland was not giving him a fair shake when it came to the major league team. After not receiving an invite to spring training in 1937, the 24-year-old wrote a letter to baseball commissioner Judge Kenesaw Mountain Landis stating his case of how the Indians were being unfair to him. The commissioner agreed and declared Henrich a free agent in early April. Less than a week after the commissioner's decision, Henrich signed with the Yankees for a yearly salary of $5,000. Henrich played seven games for the Yankees' minor league affiliate in Newark of the International League, then was brought up for good in early May.

Henrich, who played his entire 11-year major league career with the Yankees, was a five-time All-Star who played on seven Yankees world championship teams. His signature moment with the Yankees came in the 1941 World Series against the Brooklyn Dodgers. The Yankees led the Series two games to one, but trailed 4–3 in the top of the ninth of Game 4 at Ebbets Field. With two out and no one on, Henrich was the Yankees' last hope. The count was three and two when Henrich swung and missed, but the ball got past Dodgers catcher Mickey Owen to put a runner on first. Four batters later, the Yankees had a 7–4 lead and the Dodgers would never recover. The Yankees wrapped up the Series in Game 5 with a 3–1 win.

2. In the deciding Game 5 of the 2012 American League Division Series vs. the Baltimore Orioles, left-hander C.C. Sabathia went the distance for a 3–1 win.

The Yankees were comfortable with having their ace on the mound at Yankee Stadium in a do or die game. Sabathia tossed nine innings in the Series-clinching win. The 6'6" lefty gave up a run on four hits with nine strikeouts.

Sabathia signed with the Yankees as a free agent in 2009 and paid immediate dividends as he helped lead the team to its 27th world championship.

Against Minnesota in the American League Divisional Series, Sabathia won the opener with 6 2/3 innings of one-run ball. In Game 1 of the American League Championship Series vs. the Los Angeles Angels, he went eight innings and gave up one run in a 4–1 win. In Game 4, the Yankees coasted to a 10–1 win. Sabathia tossed eight innings of one-run ball.

The left-hander tossed 230 innings in the regular season, and going into the World Series against the Philadelphia Phillies he already had over 22 postseason innings. Sabathia lost Game 1, but he came back to win Game 4 to give the Yankees a three games to one lead in the Series that they won in six.

In 2010 Sabathia finished with 21 wins, but finished third in the voting for the American League's Cy Young Award. Over the next three seasons Sabathia won 48 games, but injuries curtailed his production after 2013. His velocity had diminished, so Sabathia needed to learn how to pitch without a blazing fastball. In 2016, the left-hander won nine games and finished with a respectable 3.91 ERA.

3. Tim Raines, Derek Jeter, and Paul O'Neill became the first trio to hit consecutive home runs in a postseason game.

In the bottom of the sixth of Game 1 of the American League Divisional Series vs. the Cleveland Indians, the Yankees trailed 6–4 and had a runner on first with two out. Raines faced ex-Yankees pitcher Eric Plunk and hit a mammoth two-run home run into the right field upper deck to tie the game. After Raines received a curtain call from the raucous crowd, Jeter lined an 0–2 pitch that reached the first few rows of the left field stands. Back-to-back home runs put the crowd at a fever pitch, but it wasn't over yet.

Cleveland replaced Plunk with another former Yankee, left-hander Paul Assenmacher. O'Neill fell behind 0–2, but he crushed the next pitch over the 408-foot sign in center field to complete the barrage. Jeter was in his second year, while O'Neill had already established himself as a solid presence in the Yankees' lineup.

Raines was 36 years old and a 17-year major league veteran when he joined the Yankees for the 1996 season. The switch-hitting outfielder came to New York in a trade with the Chicago White Sox during the previous offseason.

In the 1996 World Series, the switch-hitter helped the Yankees get off to a much-needed fast start in Game 3 in Atlanta. The Yankees trailed two games to none. In the top of the first, Raines walked on a 3–2 pitch from Braves starter Tom Glavine and scored the first run of the game on Bernie

Williams's RBI single. That run seemed to relax the Yankees. It provided some momentum to complete a comeback in the Series and eventually win it in six games. Raines was a four-time National League leader in stolen bases while he played with the Montreal Expos in the early 1980s, but he swiped only 26 bags during his three-year tenure with the Yankees. In February of 2000, the 40-year-old Raines signed a minor league contract, but he failed to make the team and was cut in March.

On January 18, 2017, Tim Raines was elected to baseball's Hall of Fame.

4. Former Yankees pitcher Jim Bouton is best known for authoring a revealing, behind-the-scenes look at what goes on behind closed doors in a major league clubhouse in a book entitled *Ball Four*.

The book chronicles Bouton's experiences when he was with the 1969 Seattle Pilots, but he also touched on his time with the Yankees in the early 1960s.

In his first career start in 1962, Bouton tossed a complete game, seven-hit shutout for the Yankees vs. the Washington Senators at Yankee Stadium. Bouton, who was the first Yankee to wear number 56, won 21 games in 1963 to finish second in the American League to teammate Whitey Ford, who won 24 games. In the 1963 World Series, Bouton started Game 3 in Los Angeles against the Dodgers. He gave up one run in seven innings pitched as the Yankees lost, 1–0.

Bouton won 18 games in 1964 while leading the American League with 37 starts. The Western Michigan alum won two games in the 1964 World Series against the St. Louis Cardinals. In June of 1968, Bouton's career in pinstripes came to an end when he was sold to the expansion Seattle Pilots, who would begin play in 1969.

Bouton penned his best-selling book, *Ball Four*, in 1970. During the 1969 season, Bouton spoke into a tape recorder almost every day and then sent the tapes to sportswriter Leonard Schecter, who transcribed the tapes. Bouton began the season with Seattle but was traded to the Houston Astros in August. The book's release in 1970 was met with controversy as Bouton touched on subjects that no one had previously publicized, and which were considered taboo to even acknowledge. "See no evil, hear no evil, write no evil" was the mantra around baseball clubhouses back in those days.

Bouton dared to defy his peers with a book that told about clubhouse hijinks, missing curfews, the use of amphetamines, sexual innuendos, and just about anything that went on underneath the stands. After excerpts of the book were released in June, Bouton appeared in a game in New York against the Mets and was lustily booed. *Ball Four* has been re-issued three times with updates about Bouton's life and about some of the teammates who were mentioned.

5. Robinson Cano, Russell Martin and Curtis Granderson all hit grand slam home runs in the same game to set a major league record.

In August of 2011, the Yankees were hosting the Oakland A's and were trailing 7–2 in the fifth, when Cano's blast to right-center field cut the lead to one run.

The very next inning, Martin cleared the bases with a line drive that went over the auxiliary scoreboard in right-center field and landed in the stands, as the Yankees took a 10–7 lead. Granderson capped off this amazing achievement in the eighth by taking a low pitch from A's right-hander Brian Billings and depositing it into the Yankees' bullpen in right-center field. The game was so one-sided that, in the ninth inning, catcher Jorge Posada played second base for the only time in his major league career.

Cano was a "homegrown" Yankee, while Martin and Granderson came to the Yankees as free agent signings. Martin played only two seasons with the Yankees but was a significant factor in helping to lead the team to division titles in 2011 and 2012. Posada was in his final season in 2011, so Martin was signed to take over as the starting catcher. From the start, Martin provided leadership with his defensive skills and his handling of the pitching staff. The Canadian-born Martin demonstrated a grit and toughness that resembled the late Thurman Munson.

In 2012, Martin hit a number of big home runs down the stretch to help the Yankees hold off the Baltimore Orioles and win a tight race in the American League East.

Granderson spent four seasons with the Yankees, from 2010 to 2013. The Yankees felt his left-handed bat would play well with the short right field porch at Yankee Stadium. Granderson's best season was 2011. He made the All-Star team and finished with 41 home runs and 119 runs batted in. He followed that up with 43 home runs in 2012. In Game 5 of the American League Division Series against Baltimore, Granderson hit a big home run as part of a 3–1 Series-clinching victory.

6. In the seventh game of the 1952 World Series at Brooklyn's Ebbets Field, the Yankees led the Dodgers, 4–2, in the seventh inning.

With the bases loaded and two outs, Dodgers second baseman Jackie Robinson lifted a pop fly to the right of the pitching mound. A stiff wind was blowing and it altered the flight of the ball. It looked as though the ball would drop in for a hit and two runs because the runners were going with two out. Yankee second baseman Billy Martin raced in at the last moment and made a lunging grab to snare the ball and end the inning. The catch saved the game and the Series for the Yankees.

Martin's baseball instincts made him a perfect choice to be a major league manager.

After three previous managerial stints, Martin replaced Bill Virdon as the Yankees' manager in August of 1975. In 1976, Martin led the Yankees to their first American League pennant, but they were swept by the Cincinnati Reds in the World Series.

During the offseason, Yankees owner George Steinbrenner signed free agent slugger Reggie Jackson.

A tumultuous relationship between player and manager came to a head in a nationally televised game on June 18, 1977, at Boston's Fenway Park. In the bottom of the sixth, Martin felt Jackson loafed after a ball on a base hit to right and failed to keep Boston's Jim Rice at first, so he sent Paul Blair out to replace him. When the slugger reached the dugout, he immediately confronted the manager. The whole scene was being played out on television. Jackson and Martin nearly came to blows before coach Elston Howard moved in to intervene and prevent any fisticuffs.

Despite the controversy, that season Martin piloted the Yankees to their first world championship in fifteen years. In 1978, Martin was fired after he made a derogatory comment about Jackson and Steinbrenner. The Yankees' owner brought Martin back in June of 1979, but fired him for a second time after the season. In 1983, Martin began a third tenure. The Yankees challenged the Baltimore Orioles, but came up short and Martin was once again let go. Martin had two more tenures, in 1985 and 1988. There were rumors that Martin was going to return for a sixth tenure, but he died in 1989 in a tragic car accident on Christmas Day.

7. He was known as "Super Chief" because his mother was a Creek Indian, and Allie Reynolds was indeed pretty "super" during his eight-year Yankee career.

The Yankees acquired the 6', 195-pound right-hander from Cleveland in October of 1946 for Hall of Fame second baseman Joe Gordon. The Indians wanted Gordon so badly they told the Yankees they could have any pitcher in return, except for Hall of Famer Bob Feller. The 30-year-old hard throwing right-hander had a stellar season in 1947, his first in New York, as he posted a 19–8 record with a 3.20 ERA. He was especially good in helping the Yankees win six world championships, including five in a row from 1949 to 1953. In 1951, Reynolds did something that no Yankee pitcher did before, or has done since. Reynolds put his name in the franchise record books by tossing two no-hitters in the same season. The first came on July 12th against the Indians at Cleveland's Municipal Stadium. Reynolds was matched up with Feller, who was brilliant in his own right, so scoring was at a premium.

In the top of the seventh, Yankees center fielder Gene Woodling homered off Feller for what turned out to be the only run of the game. Reynolds took it from there as he set down the last 17 hitters to record his first career no-hitter, but he wasn't finished yet. On September 28th, in the opening game of a doubleheader at Yankee Stadium, Reynolds no-hit the Boston

Red Sox, 8–0. It was the second time in major league history that a pitcher had thrown two no-hitters in the same season (Cincinnati Reds pitcher Johnny Vander Meer threw back-to-back no-hit games in 1938), but it almost didn't happen.

Reynolds faced Hall of Famer Ted Williams with two out in the ninth and got him to hit a pop-up behind the plate. Catcher Yogi Berra dropped it for an error, and Williams had another chance to break up the no-hit bid. On the very next pitch, Reynolds got Williams to hit the same foul pop-up behind the plate, and this time Berra held on to the ball to preserve history.

8. A total of 13 Yankees managers have also played for the team.

Three were Hall of Fame players, including Yogi Berra, Bill Dickey, and Frank Chance, who was the Yankees' first manager, in 1913.

Frank Chance played for the Yankees and was their first manager. (Library of Congress)

The popular Yogi Berra had two tenures as Yankees skipper. The first was in 1964, when he led the Yankees to the American League pennant but lost the World Series in seven games to the St. Louis Cardinals. Berra was fired after the season.

The three-time American League Most Valuable Player returned to pilot the team in 1984, but was let go in a controversial move just 16 games into the 1985 season.

Bill Dickey took over the reins after Joe McCarthy resigned midway through the 1946 season, but stepped down in September and finished out his final season as a player only.

Ralph Houk also served two tenures, and has managed the most games of those who were also former players. Houk, a former Army Ranger whose nickname was "the Major," replaced Casey Stengel for the 1961 season, and led the Yankees to the world championship. Houk won again in 1962, but lost a four-game sweep in 1963 to the Los Angeles Dodgers the following season. The native of Lawrence, Kansas, moved into the front office as general manager in 1964, but returned to the dugout beginning with the 1966 season. Houk left the organization following the 1973 season.

Billy Martin had five separate tenures as Yankees manager.

Roger Peckinpaugh replaced Chance late in the 1914 season and managed for only 20 games.

"Wild" Bill Donovan was a player-manager for the Yankees for three seasons, from 1915 to 1917.

Bob Shawkey is known more for being the first starting pitcher at the original Yankee Stadium, but he managed the team for one season, in 1930.

Dick Howser managed the team for one season, in 1980, and won 103 games and the American League's Eastern

Division title. He lost the American League Championship Series to the Kansas City Royals and was fired after one season. Gene Michael, Lou Piniella, and Bucky Dent were also former players who served as the Yankees manager. Current manager Joe Girardi rounds out the exclusive list.

9. The horrific terrorist attacks that rocked New York City and the Pentagon on September 11, 2001, put the 2001 season on hold.

Ten days later, the season resumed. That meant the World Series could extend into the month of November for the first time.

The Yankees played the Arizona Diamondbacks in that year's Fall Classic. In Games 4 and 5, the Yankees became the first team to stage ninth inning comebacks in consecutive World Series games, as Tino Martinez and Scott Brosius both hit game-tying two-run home runs. The Yankees trailed the Series two games to one and were down to their final out in Game 4. Arizona had a 3–1 lead in the ninth, but the Yankees had the tying run at the plate. Martinez faced Diamondbacks closer Byung-Hyun Kim and drove his first pitch over the right-center field wall for a game-tying, two-run home run. Yankee Stadium was literally shaking as Martinez circled the bases. Derek Jeter's walkoff home run in the bottom of the 10th gave the Yankees a 4–3 win to even the Series at two games apiece.

Jeter's home run came after the stroke of midnight on November 1st, making it the first major league baseball ever played in the 11th month of the year. With two out and a man on, the Yankees again trailed by two in the bottom of the ninth of Game 5 and were facing the Arizona closer once again. This time, Brosius whacked a 1–0 pitch into the left field stands for a second consecutive game-tying home run in the ninth.

Alfonso Soriano's walkoff, RBI single in the bottom of the 12th enabled the Yankees to score a 3–2 win.

Martinez was acquired in a trade with Seattle to replace Don Mattingly. The Tampa, Florida, native had a bit of a tough time early in his Yankee career, but eventually he won the fans over to become a productive player during his seven years with the Yankees.

Following the 1997 season, the Yankees acquired Brosius from the Oakland A's. In 1998, Brosius capped off a very successful first season with the team by winning the World Series Most Valuable Player Award. During the four-game sweep vs San Diego, Brosius batted .471, with two home runs and six runs batted in. He retired as a Yankee following the 2001 season.

10. In Game 4 of the 2001 American League Championship Series vs. the Seattle Mariners, second baseman Alfonso Soriano hit a two-run, walkoff home run to give the Yankees a 3–1 win and a three games to one lead in the best-of-seven series.

With the game knotted at one in the bottom of the ninth, Scott Brosius singled with one out. Seattle had its closer, Kazuhiro Sasaki, on the mound to try and get the game into extra innings. Soriano drove a 1–0 pitch into the bleachers, to the right of the 385-foot sign in right-center field, giving the Yankees a 3–1 victory.

As a 21-year-old, Soriano had begun his pro career in Japan, where he played in only nine games. Things didn't work out for him in Japan, so he "retired" and made himself available to the American major league teams. The "retirement" was part of a contractual ploy that upset his Japanese team, the Carp, which threatened to sue. A few years earlier, Japanese pitching star Hideo Nomo had retired and then returned to baseball a year later to sign with the Los Angeles Dodgers.

Soriano's combination of speed and power made him attractive to a number of clubs. Reportedly, the Indians were very interested in Soriano, so the Yankees more than doubled Cleveland's offer to five years at $3.1 million.

In September of 1999, the native of San Pedro de Macoris in the Dominican Republic made his first major league home run a memorable one. In his third major league at-bat, Soriano hit a game-winning, walkoff home run in the bottom of the 11th inning to beat the Tampa Bay Devil Rays, 4–3.

In 2002, Soriano had his best season in pinstripes; he was named an All-Star and finished third in the voting for the American League's Most Valuable Player Award.

His numbers were off the charts:
- .300 batting average
- 209 hits
- 39 home runs
- 102 runs batted in
- 128 runs scored
- 41 stolen bases

Soriano played one more season for the Yankees before becoming part of a famous trade. The second baseman was dealt to the Texas Rangers in February of 2004 for Alex Rodriguez.

11. In early September of 1964, the Yankees were in third place in the American League, two-and-a-half games behind the first place Chicago White Sox.

The Yankees bullpen was having its problems, so they desperately needed to add an arm for the stretch run. On September 5th, the Yankees acquired right-handed reliever Pedro Ramos from the Cleveland Indians for two players to be named later. (Pitchers Ralph Terry and Bud Daley went to Cleveland to complete the deal.)

Since Ramos was acquired after September 1st, he would not be eligible for the World Series. No matter, as he played an important role down the stretch to help the Yankees win the American League pennant and get into the Series.

Ramos made 13 appearances in a critical month of September, when he won one game and saved eight others. The Cuba-born right-hander made his Yankees debut on September 6th in Kansas City and recorded his first save as a Yankee. In a mid-September game, Yankees ace pitcher Whitey Ford was having arm problems. Ford started against the Minnesota Twins, but had to leave the game after four innings because his arm was feeling numb. Ramos relieved the Yankee left-hander and tossed five scoreless innings to get the win in a pivotal 5–2 win. The 29-year-old was a workhorse in the final weeks of the season. On September 23rd, Ramos saved both ends of a doubleheader sweep against his old team, the Indians, at Cleveland Stadium. The Yankees were on a nine-game winning streak that catapulted them to four games in front of the Orioles with 10 games to play. On the penultimate day of the season, the Cuban righty was on the mound as the Yankees clinched the American League pennant with an 8–3 win over the Indians. Ramos was credited with a save (requirements for a save were different in 1964) that gave him eight as the Yankees went 22–6 in September. By rule, Ramos was not on the World Series roster as the Yankees lost to the St. Louis Cardinals in seven games.

Many observers pointed to that absence as the possible reason the Yankees lost the Series.

12. In the 30th round of the 1988 amateur draft, the Yankees selected an outfielder from Florida State named Deion Sanders.

The 21-year-old was a two-sport (baseball and football) star in college, but the Yankees still signed Sanders with the hope he would stick with baseball. He played 28 games in the minors in 1988 before going back to school. In April of 1989, the Atlanta Falcons selected him as the fifth overall pick in the NFL Draft. On June 4th, Sanders hit his first major league home run. He was sent back to the minors a week later and was recalled in September.

In early September, Sanders played six innings in a game in Seattle, hit a home run, and then abruptly left the team to join the Falcons of the National Football League. Four days after leaving the Yankees, Sanders scored a touchdown against the Los Angeles Rams on a 68-yard punt return. Sanders became the first player in history to hit a major league home run and score an NFL touchdown in the same week.

In July of 1990, Sanders electrified the home crowd with an exciting inside-the-park home run against Kansas City at Yankee Stadium. With a man on and one out, Sanders drove a pitch toward right-center field that got past Royals center fielder Bo Jackson (another two-sport star). The speedy Sanders was off to the races. As Sanders headed for home, the relay throw beat him but skipped past Royals catcher Mike Macfarlane. As Macfarlane was making a move for the ball he flipped Sanders up in the air, which caused the Yankee speedster to miss the plate. Royals rookie pitcher Mel Stottlemyre Jr. was backing up the play and tossed the ball to Macfarlane, who couldn't handle it. Sanders was then able to get his hand on the plate and was called safe.

Sanders left the team in late July to join the Falcons once again. Frustrated by his lack of commitment to baseball, the Yankees gave Sanders his unconditional release in September.

13. In 1998, the Yankees' designated hitter Darryl Strawberry became the fourth player in major league history to hit two pinch-hit grand slam home runs in the same season.

The first came on May 2nd at Kansas City. Strawberry was batting for catcher Joe Girardi in the top of the ninth. The Yankees' pinch-hitter cleared the bases with a home run off Royals pitcher Scott Service to complete the scoring in a 12–6 win. The second time was in late August. In the second game of a doubleheader in Oakland, the Yankees trailed, 5–1, in the top of the ninth, but loaded the bases with nobody out. Once again, Strawberry hit for Girardi and, for a second time, he delivered a pinch-hit grand slam that tied the game.

The New York Mets had selected Strawberry as the #1 overall pick of the 1980 amateur draft. The highly touted outfielder made his major league debut in 1983 and was named the National League Rookie of the Year. Following the 1990 season, Strawberry left the Mets as a free agent and signed with his hometown Los Angeles Dodgers. The homecoming didn't quite work out; Strawberry was dealing with personal issues off the field. The slugger was drinking and using drugs, and was going through a very messy divorce, so the Dodgers cut ties with the left-handed hitter after he was released from a rehab clinic in May of 1994. A little over a month later he signed with the San Francisco Giants, but was released the following spring.

Yankees owner George Steinbrenner signed Strawberry in July of 1995; he made his Yankee debut the following month. After the 1996 season began, the Yankees re-signed the 6'6" free agent slugger, who joined the team in July. And by August Strawberry reverted back to his younger days by slamming three home runs against the Chicago White Sox at Yankee Stadium. In the five-game ALCS series win over Baltimore, Strawberry batted .417 with three home runs and five runs batted in.

In 1998, Strawberry was diagnosed with cancer and missed the postseason. After undergoing cancer treatments and serving a 140-game Major League Baseball–mandated suspension for cocaine use and soliciting an undercover police officer for sex, Strawberry returned to the Yankees in September of 1999 and retired after the season.

14. In December of 1975, the Yankees traded outfielder Bobby Bonds to the California Angels in exchange for speedy outfielder Mickey Rivers and right-handed pitcher Ed Figueroa.

It turned into one of the best trades in Yankees history. Yankees president Gabe Paul sided with manager Billy Martin in that the lineup needed more speed. Martin liked Figueroa, so Bonds was used as trade bait. The 27-year-old Rivers added another dimension to the Yankees offense. Figueroa got his first Yankees win in the second game at the remodeled Yankee Stadium. The righty tossed a complete game, six-hit shutout as the Yankees routed the Minnesota Twins, 10–0. Rivers gave the Yankees everything they had hoped for; he was an immediate hit with the fans. When "Mick the Quick" walked to the plate he would look like his legs hurt all over, but there he was speeding down the line to leg out a bunt hit. When he swung and missed at a pitch, Rivers would "twirl" his bat and adopt an awkward looking stance.

With Rivers and Figueroa added to the roster in 1976, the Yankees won their first American League pennant in 12 years. In the American League Championship Series against the Kansas City Royals, Martin started Figueroa in the do or die Game 5 at Yankee Stadium. The right-hander pitched seven innings and left with a 6–4 lead, but got a "no decision" when the Royals eventually tied the game on Hall of Famer George Brett's three-run homer in the eighth. Rivers was spectacular against the Royals. The spark plug of the Yankees lineup batted .348 and scored five runs in five games. In Game 5, Rivers had three hits and scored three runs. In the World Series, Figueroa started Game 4 but couldn't hold off the powerful Cincinnati Reds, who completed a four-game sweep. The Reds knew they had to keep Rivers off base. Third baseman Pete Rose wanted to not only take the bunt away, he wanted to get into Rivers's head by moving to within 65 feet of the batter. The ploy worked as Rivers was held to three hits in 18 at-bats for a .167 average.

In 1978, Figueroa became the first Puerto Rico–born pitcher to win 20 games in the major leagues. In July of 1980, he was sold to the Texas Rangers. Rivers was traded to Texas in July of 1979.

15. Hall of Fame shortstop Phil Rizzuto holds the Yankees' franchise record for the most stolen bases in World Series play with 10.

One of those steals helped the Yankees win Game 3 of the 1950 World Series against the Philadelphia Phillies. With the game scoreless in the third, Rizzuto singled, stole second, and ended up at third on a wild throw from Phils catcher Andy Seminick. Yankees second baseman Jerry Coleman singled to left to score Rizzuto with the first run en route to a 3–2 win.

Rizzuto was a 5'6", 150-pound infielder who had been told he was too short to play in the big leagues. Going into the 1941 season, Brooklyn-born Rizzuto was the heir apparent to shortstop Frank Crosetti, but the veteran players resented the rookie who was threatening to replace one of their own. Joe DiMaggio intervened and Rizzuto was eventually accepted by the rest of the team. In the 1947 World Series, Rizzuto hit .308 and was a key player in the seventh and deciding game at Yankee Stadium. "The Scooter" had three hits and scored twice as the Yankees took the final game and the Series with a 5–2 win.

Rizzuto's standout season was 1950, when he hit .324, scored 125 runs, and was named the AL MVP. He was a pivotal player on the Yankees team that won five straight world championships, from 1949 to 1953. In the clinching Game 6 of the 1953 World Series, Rizzuto had two hits and scored a run in the Yankees' 4–3 win.

In August of 1956, the Yankees released Rizzuto. The 38-year-old was stunned by the news, but little did he realize that he would be starting a whole new career as a broadcaster. Beginning in 1957, Rizzuto worked alongside legendary broadcasters Mel Allen and Red Barber, calling the Yankees games. Rizzuto became popular with generations of fans for his catchphrase, "Holy cow!," and his relationship with Bill White, his broadcasting partner for many years. Rizzuto's uniform number 10 was retired by the Yankees in 1985. He was elected to Baseball's Hall of Fame by the Veterans Committee in 1994.

16. Tony Lazzeri became the first Yankee to hit a World Series grand slam. The milestone occurred in Game 2 of the 1936 World Series against the crosstown New York Giants at the Polo Grounds.

In the third inning of Game 5 of the 1951 World Series at the Polo Grounds, Yankees rookie second baseman Gil McDougald hit a grand slam to key a five-run inning.

The Yankees lost two World Series in which they hit grand slam home runs. Bobby Richardson's World Series grand slam in the 1960 World Series provided four of his record-setting 12 runs batted in. Richardson became the only player from a losing team to win the World Series MVP award.

Joe Pepitone became the seventh Yankee to hit a World Series grand slam home run when he cleared the bases in Game 6 of the 1964 World Series vs. the St. Louis Cardinals.

In Game 5 of the 1953 World Series, the Yankees had the bases loaded with Mickey Mantle at the plate. Dodgers manager Chuck Dressen elected to turn Mantle around to bat from his left side, so he replaced left-hander Johnny Podres with right-hander Russ Meyer. The move backfired with one pitch as Mantle unloaded on a curveball and planted it in the upper deck.

In the 1956 Series, the Yankees hit two grand slams. Yogi Berra's slam off Dodgers pitcher and Hall of Famer Don Newcombe came in the second inning of Game 2, but the Dodgers won, 13–8. In the seventh game, first baseman Bill "Moose" Skowron delivered one of his biggest hits as a Yankee. Moose hit a seventh inning grand slam home run off Dodgers right-hander Roger Craig to cap the scoring in a 9–0 win.

In Game 1 of the 1998 World Series against the San Diego Padres at Yankee Stadium, Tino Martinez hit a controversial grand slam. On a 2–2 pitch, it appeared that Padres pitcher Mark Langston had Martinez struck out, but home plate umpire Rich Garcia called it a ball. The Yankees' first baseman drove the next pitch into the upper deck in right field to snap a 5–5 tie and give the Yankees a 9–6 win.

17. In 1977, Yankees closer Sparky Lyle became the first relief pitcher to win the American League Cy Young Award.

Lyle appeared in 72 games and had 26 saves to head the bullpen as the Yankees won their first World Series in 15 years. The colorful left-hander was acquired from the Boston Red Sox in exchange for first baseman Danny Cater and a player to be named later in the spring of 1972. In his very first game in pinstripes the Yankees were leading the Milwaukee Brewers, 3–2, with two out in the top of the ninth at Yankee Stadium. Manager Ralph Houk brought in Lyle to face Milwaukee's slugging third baseman George Scott. The closer got the slugging right-handed hitter to ground out to second for Lyle's first save as a Yankee.

With a biting slider as his out pitch, the native of DuBois, Pennsylvania, saved 35 games in 1972 to set a record for left-handed relievers. Thanks in part to Lyle, in 1972 the Yankees were a factor in the divisional race for the first time since the sport had expanded to a two-division format in each league in 1969. On August 10th the Yankees, who trailed Detroit by three games for first place, led the Tigers, 1–0. In the ninth inning, Detroit had runners on second and third with two out. Lyle intentionally walked Willie Horton, and then struck out pinch-hitter Ike Brown with the bases loaded to end the game, sending the crowd of over 45,000 into a frenzy. The win moved the Yankees to within two games of Detroit, but they fizzled down the stretch and finished in fourth place.

Lyle was traditionally brought in from the bullpen in a car while "Pomp and Circumstance" (the ceremonial theme that is played at graduations) played over the stadium loudspeaker.

In 1978 the Yankees signed free agent closer Rich "Goose" Gossage, and Lyle was deemed expendable. After the season, the Yankees traded Lyle to the Texas Rangers as part of a nine-player trade. Lefty pitcher Dave Righetti was part of the package that the Yankees got back in the deal.

18. In 1975, the Yankees hosted the Minnesota Twins in a game that began at Shea Stadium but ended in Minneapolis.

After the Twins batted in the top of the 14th of a 6–6 tie, the game at Shea was suspended due to an American League–mandated curfew rule that was in effect. (No inning could start after 1 a.m.) Since it was Minnesota's last trip into New York that season, it was decided that the game would be completed in Minneapolis a week later. A wild ninth inning helped create this scenario. The Twins scored four runs in the top of the ninth to take a 6–3 lead, but the Yankees rallied to tie the game on Thurman Munson's two-out, RBI single. When the game resumed on July 19th at Metropolitan Stadium, the Yankees were wearing their "road gray" uniforms. A whole new four-man crew was brought in to replace the four umpires who had worked the game at Shea Stadium.

The Twins took a 7–6 lead in the top of the 16th inning on a two-out, RBI single by pinch-hitter Tom Lundstedt, *who had been in the minor leagues when the game actually began!* The Yankees had "last licks" in this road game, and they made good use of their final at-bat. With one out, back-to-back singles by Roy White and Thurman Munson put runners on first and second. After a forceout at second, Graig Nettles tied the game with a two-out single. With runners at first and third, Lou Piniella singled to right field to drive in the winning run.

In the Shea Stadium portion of the game, Munson had an RBI single nullified by home plate umpire Art Frantz in the first inning. The Twins claimed Munson had too much pine tar on his bat and that made it illegal. Frantz measured the bat and called Munson out in an eerie portent of things to come eight years later in the "Pine Tar" game against Kansas City.

19. The longest winning streak in Yankees franchise history is 19 straight games, in 1947.

The streak began on June 29th with a 3–1 win over the Washington Senators in the second game of a doubleheader at Griffith Stadium. The next day, the Yankees beat the Red Sox 3–1 in a one-game appearance at Fenway Park. The Yankees returned home and swept a six-game home stand against the Senators and Philadelphia Athletics for their eighth win in a row. Following the All-Star break, the Yankees began a 15-game road trip with a four-game series vs. the St. Louis Browns at Sportsman's Park. The Yankees and lowly Browns were tied at three in the top of the ninth. Yankee relief pitcher Joe Page snapped the tie with a solo home run, and then retired St. Louis in order in the bottom of the ninth to earn the win with his arm and his bat.

The Yankees completed a sweep of the four-game series by taking both ends of a doubleheader to make it 12 straight wins. The very next day, the Yankees played a second consecutive doubleheader in Chicago against the White Sox. In the opener the White Sox took a 3–0 first inning lead, but the Yankees scored 10 unanswered runs to win, 10–3. The Yankees won the second game, 6–4, for their 14th consecutive win. Following a day off, the Yankees traveled to Cleveland for a third straight doubleheader and swept both games to tie the franchise record of 16 straight wins set in 1926.

On July 16th, the Yankees set a new team record as they beat the Indians, 8–2, to make it 17 straight wins. The next day, the Yankees and Indians played another doubleheader to conclude a five-game series. In Game 1, 39-year-old veteran pitcher Bobo Newsom, who had been purchased by the Yankees from the Senators just six days earlier, tossed a complete game for his 200th career win as the Yankees beat Cleveland, 3–1. A 7–2 win in the second game, keyed by a complete game from right-hander Vic Raschi, gave the Yankees their 19th consecutive victory.

The streak ended on July 18th at Detroit's Briggs Stadium with an 8–0 loss.

20. The Yankees led the Pittsburgh Pirates, 7–4, in Game 7 of the 1960 World Series when a bad hop single, which struck Yankees shortstop Tony Kubek in the adam's apple, turned the game and the Series.

After a leadoff single by Pittsburgh's Gino Cimoli, the Bucs' Bill Virdon (who would later become a Yankees manager) hit a bouncer toward shortstop. Kubek was in position to field the ball and start a doubleplay, but as a result of one of the many divots in the Forbes Field infield, it took a bad hop and knocked him to the ground.

Following the freak play, Pittsburgh went on to score five times, capped off by a three-run home run by back-up catcher Hal Smith to take a 9–7 lead into the ninth. The Yankees tied it in the top of the ninth, only to lose on Bill Mazeroski's famous walkoff home run.

The Pirates' Bill Mazeroski rounds the bases after his walkoff home run against the Yankees to win the 1960 World Series. (Photo courtesy of the Pittsburgh Pirates)

Kubek made his debut in 1957 as a versatile player who manned four positions. He batted .297 and was named the American League Rookie of the Year. Kubek took over the everyday shortstop job in 1958. The incumbent, Gil McDougald, was moved to second base to form a potent doubleplay combination.

Following the Yankees' World Series win over the Milwaukee Braves in seven games, Kubek served time with the U.S. Army Reserve. He rejoined the Yankees 10 days before the start of the 1959 season, after receiving an early discharge. Kubek became the everyday shortstop once again in 1960. In 1961, he set a Yankees single-season record for short-stops with 38 doubles. After the Yankees won the 1961 World Series, Kubek served a second stint in the military. He missed the first four months of the 1962 season and did not re-join the team until early August. Kubek retired after the 1965 season after it was discovered he had nerve damage at the top of his spinal cord.

21. Alex Rodriguez is the only player in franchise history to hit two home runs in one inning twice.

On September 5, 2007, the Yankees hosted the Seattle Mariners at Yankee Stadium. In the bottom of the seventh, Rodriguez led off the inning with his 48th home run of the season off Mariners left-hander Jarrod Washburn. The Yankees batted around, and in his second at-bat of the inning A-Rod faced Seattle right-handed relief pitcher Brandon Morrow. Rodriguez drove a ball deep into the left field stands to become the fourth Yankee in franchise history to hit two home runs in one inning.

On October 4, 2009, the Yankees played the Rays in Tampa on the final day of the regular season. In the top of the sixth, Rodriguez hit a three-run homer to give the Yankees a 3–1 lead. The inning would continue until the Yankees had a 6–1 lead, when Rodriguez came to the plate for his second at-bat, this time with the bases loaded. A-Rod cleared the bases for his eighth grand slam home run as a Yankee, and the 17th of his career.

In February of 2004, the Yankees had acquired Rodri-guez from the Texas Rangers in exchange for second baseman

Alfonso Soriano and a player to be named later. Derek Jeter was ensconced at shortstop, so A-Rod agreed to play third base.

Rodriguez put up some impressive numbers during his 12 years with the Yankees. He was a seven-time All-Star and two-time MVP. In 2007, he put together one of the greatest single seasons in franchise history. Rodriguez slammed 54 home runs and drove in 156, with a slash line of .314/.422/.645, and an OPS of 1.067.

Rodriguez had his best postseason as a Yankee in 2009, when he was a key player during the championship run. In 15 postseason games, including the World Series, Rodriguez had six home runs and 18 runs batted in to lead the Yankees to their 27th world championship. Rodriguez served a season-long suspension in 2014 for violating Major League Baseball's drug policy.

A-Rod announced his retirement in August of 2016.

22. Hall of Famer Dave Winfield is the only other Yankee, besides Derek Jeter, to have three hits in an All-Star Game.

In the 1983 All-Star Game at Chicago's Comiskey Park, Winfield started in right field and was 3 for 3 with two runs scored as the American League beat the National League, 13–3, to snap an 11-game losing streak.

The San Diego Padres chose the versatile athlete with the fourth overall pick of the 1973 amateur draft. The 6'6" Winfield was chosen by the NBA's Atlanta Hawks, the Utah Stars of the ABA, and the Minnesota Vikings of the NFL in their respective drafts. Winfield bypassed a minor league stint and debuted with the San Diego Padres as a 21-year-old in June of 1973. In December of 1980, he signed a record-setting free agent contract to join the Yankees. The University of

Minnesota product became the highest paid player in baseball when he inked a 10-year, $23 million contract that featured an annual cost of living increase.

Winfield was brought in to take the mantle from Reggie Jackson, who was in the final year of his contract. In the 1981 World Series, Winfield batted .045 in the Yankees' six-game series loss to the Los Angeles Dodgers. When Winfield got his one hit in the series, he kiddingly asked for the ball. Yankees owner George Steinbrenner always put a lot of pressure on his highest paid player to produce, so when the Series was over he did not take kindly to the gesture and publicly criticized his star player. This was the beginning of their feud that reached its climax a number of years later.

Beginning in 1982, Winfield drove in 100 or more runs in six of the next seven seasons. The Yankees failed to win a division title during that time and Steinbrenner pinned the blame on Winfield for the championship drought. The Yankee owner's bitterness also extended from the contract that Winfield signed. Winfield missed the entire 1989 season due to a back injury. In May of 1990, Winfield agreed to be traded to the California Angels for pitcher Mike Witt.

23. The Yankees have retired 20 uniform numbers in honor of 21 players.

It began with Lou Gehrig's number 4, which was officially retired on January 6th, 1940, without a ceremony (the announcement was made by team president Ed Barrow), and then Babe Ruth's number 3 in 1948.

In Yankee Stadium, the numbers are displayed in Monument Park in the order they were retired. At the home opener in 1952, the first since Joe DiMaggio announced his retirement

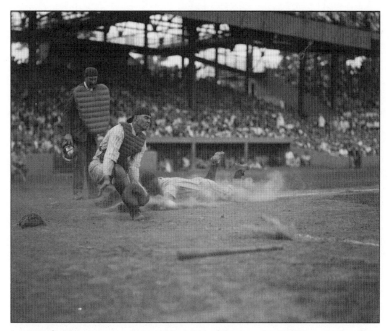

Lou Gehrig, seen scoring against Washington in 1925, was the first Yankee to have his number retired. (Library of Congress)

in 1951, the Yankees made his number 5 the third retired number. The fourth number was retired on June 8, 1969. It was Mickey Mantle Day at Yankee Stadium. The Yankees retired the Mick's number 7 in a lavish and memorable ceremony between games of a doubleheader before more than 60,000 fans. On August 8, 1970, the Yankees staged their annual Old Timers' Day and made former manager Casey Stengel's number 37 the fifth number to be retired by the Yankees. During his 12-year Yankee tenure, the "Ol Perfesser" won 10 American League pennants and seven world championships.

In 1972, the Yankees retired number 8 for two players, Yogi Berra and Bill Dickey.

On Old Timers' Day in 1974, the Yankees retired Whitey Ford's number 16. Thurman Munson's untimely death in 1979 prompted the immediate retirement of his number 15. In 1984, the Yankees again used Old Timers' Day to retire two separate numbers, Elston Howard's number 32 and Roger Maris's number 9. On Phil Rizzuto Day in 1985, the Yankees retired his number 10. Billy Martin's number 1 went up on the wall in Monument Park in 1986, followed by Reggie Jackson's number 44 in 1993 and Don Mattingly's number 23 four years later. Ron Guidry's number 49 was next in 2003. Mariano Rivera's number 42 was retired by Major League Baseball in 1997 in honor of Jackie Robinson. Rivera was allowed to wear it until he retired in 2013. On September 22nd, it was Mariano Rivera Day and the Yankees officially retired his number.

In 2014, Joe Torre became the second Yankee manager to be honored when his number 6 was retired. In 2015 there were three more numbers retired. Bernie Williams's number 51 was retired in May. Jorge Posada's number 20 was retired on August 22nd, while Andy Pettitte's number 46 was retired the very next day. Derek Jeter's number 2 will be retired during the 2017 season.

24. The final baseball game at the original Yankee Stadium took place on September 30, 1973.

The Yankees would play the 1974 and 1975 seasons at Shea Stadium in Queens, New York, while the famous building underwent a complete renovation.

Tigers right-hander Fred Holdsworth and Yankees left-hander Fritz Peterson accounted for the final starting pitching matchup before 32,238 fans. In the bottom of the seventh,

Yankees catcher Duke Sims hit the final home run of the Stadium's 51-year existence. Sims was a journeyman catcher who played a total of nine games in parts of two seasons with the Yankees. Sims's home run (the only one he would hit with the Yankees) tied the game at 2.

In the top of the eighth, the Tigers scored six runs to take an 8–4 lead. In the bottom of the eighth, Yankee second baseman Hal Lanier doubled in a run for the final hit in the history of the ballpark. The Yankees' last at-bat in the ninth came against Tigers closer John Hiller, who was credited with the final winning decision. First baseman Mike Hegan made the final out when he flied out to Tigers center fielder Mickey Stanley.

At 4:41 p.m. Eastern Time, Yankee Stadium closed for business. After the game was over, manager Ralph Houk made the stunning announcement that he was going to resign. Houk was reportedly upset over the booing he was receiving toward the end of the 1973 season. The Yankees were in first place in late July, but faded as they went 20–34 in the final third of the season to finish 17 games behind, in fourth place. George Steinbrenner was in his first year as the owner; he pressured Houk while the Yankees were falling apart down the stretch. In December, Houk announced that he was going to become the manager of the Detroit Tigers. Steinbrenner petitioned American League president Joe Cronin to award the team a form of compensation, claiming Houk was still bound to the Yankees. Cronin ruled that Houk was not legally bound to the Yankees, so he was free to sign with Detroit.

25. Twenty-three years after last playing there as a home team, the Yankees returned to Shea Stadium for a one-game cameo appearance in 1998.

A structural failure at Yankee Stadium caused the first two games of a three-game series against the Anaheim Angels to be postponed. During the afternoon of the scheduled first game, a 500-pound steel joint fell an estimated 40 feet and slammed into the mezzanine section down the left field line between third base and the outfield. Luckily no one was hurt, but the building was deemed to be unsafe until it could be thoroughly inspected.

Major League Baseball decided to move the final game of the series to Shea Stadium. The New York Mets were scheduled to play the Chicago Cubs at night, so a unique doubleheader of baseball in New York would begin just after noon on April 15, 1998. The Yankees were fully dressed in their uniforms when they left Yankee Stadium in three buses that were accompanied by a police escort. The Yankees occupied the visitors' dugout along the third base side, while the Angels used the Mets' dugout.

Famed P.A. announcer Bob Sheppard made his usual array of announcements while competing with the noise of planes going overhead. Former Met Darryl Strawberry was the Yankees' designated hitter. "Straw" hit a monstrous home run off of Angels reliever Omar Olivares in the fourth inning that traveled an estimated 402 feet. As if he was still wearing a Mets uniform, the "Apple" in center field that pops up when the home team hits a home run began to rise from the huge top hat where it's located. The operator immediately recognized his mistake and stopped it.

The Yankees beat the Angels, 6–3, before a lunch time crowd of more than 40,000 fans. Jeff Nelson relieved David Wells in the ninth with the tying run on deck and earned the save. The Yankees had an upcoming weekend series scheduled at Yankee Stadium against the Tigers, but that was moved to Detroit because of the still ongoing Yankee Stadium repairs.

The Mets beat the Cubs, 2–1, in that night's game at Shea Stadium to make it a clean sweep for the New York teams.

26. Reggie Jackson hit a solo home run that proved to be the deciding run as the Yankees beat the Boston Red Sox at Fenway Park, 5–4, in a one-game playoff for the American League Eastern Division title.

Bucky Dent's famous three-run home run was the turning point, but the Yankees would still need more to secure the win. In the eighth, with the Yankees leading 4–2, Jackson launched a ball into the center field bleachers off Red Sox pitcher Bob Stanley, for a 5–2 lead. Jackson was one of the most colorful and enigmatic players to ever put on a Yankees uniform. He had signed as a free agent in November of 1976. The signing was met with great fanfare but Jackson found himself in the middle of a tumultuous and controversial first season in New York. It began with comments that Jackson made for a national magazine article that disrespected Yankees catcher and captain Thurman Munson. This alienated the slugger and caused friction with his teammates in the early months of the season. Jackson clashed with manager Billy Martin, a problem that came to a head during a game in June on national television (see answer number 6).

In August, the Hall of Famer was moved to the cleanup spot in the batting order, and as he took off so did the Yankees.

But in the American League Championship Series against Kansas City, Jackson was struggling. Martin made a controversial decision to bench the slugger in the fifth and deciding game because the Royals were starting left-hander Paul Splittorff. Jackson was sent up to pinch-hit in the eighth inning and delivered an RBI single that cut the Royals' lead to 3–2.

The Yankees rallied in the ninth to win the American League pennant and faced the Los Angeles Dodgers in the World Series, in which Jackson delivered a performance for the ages.

The left-handed slugger hit three home runs in a memorable Series-clinching Game 6, and was named the World Series Most Valuable Player, as the Yankees won their first world championship in 15 years.

During his five-year tenure in New York, Jackson helped lead the Yankees to three pennants and two world championships. His number 44 was retired in 1993, the same year he was inducted into the Hall of Fame.

27. In 1979, Cliff Johnson and Rich "Goose" Gossage were involved in an altercation that helped derail the Yankees' chances at a third straight world championship.

After a loss to the Orioles in early April, Gossage was tossing his socks into the hamper but inadvertently grazed Johnson's shoulder. At that point, one of the other players (reportedly Reggie Jackson) baited Johnson by asking him "how well he hit Gossage when he [Johnson] played in the National League." Gossage answered first by saying, "Man can't hit what he can't see."

"Goose" was 6'3" and 215 pounds while Johnson stood at 6'4" and 225 pounds, so any physical confrontation would be comparable to a heavyweight fight. The fisticuffs began when both men reached the shower. There were reports that six or seven blows were exchanged, and some landed on the heads of both participants. Gossage missed nearly three months with torn ligaments in his right thumb as a result of the melee. After the incident, Johnson was traded to the Cleveland Indians on June 15th. Gossage returned in July but was limited to 18 saves, his lowest total as a Yankee. The hard-throwing right-hander had been signed as a free agent to take over the closer role in 1978. He replaced 1977 AL Cy Young Award winner Sparky Lyle, because Yankees owner George Steinbrenner wanted a power pitcher in that role.

When the Yankees were making their historic comeback against the Boston Red Sox in 1978, Gossage had two signature moments. In early September, Gossage was brought into a one-run game with the bases loaded and nobody out in the ninth inning against the Seattle Mariners. Goose proceeded to strike out the side to save a big win. The other was the one-game playoff against the Red Sox at Fenway Park when Gossage got Hall of Famer Carl Yastrzemski to pop out to third with the tying and winning runs on base. The hard-throwing right-hander played six full seasons with the Yankees before leaving after the 1983 season as a free agent. He returned for a short stint in 1989.

28. In June of 1957, the Yankees acquired a slick fielding third baseman from the Kansas City Athletics named Clete Boyer.

In 1960 he was assimilated into the regular lineup, playing 93 games at third base and 20 at shortstop. In the 1960 World Series, Boyer had a problem with manager Casey Stengel, whom he felt wasn't giving him a fair shake. In Game 1, Boyer started at third base but never got an at-bat.

The Yankees trailed 3–1 in the second inning. With two men on and no one out, Stengel made a surprise move when he sent up Dale Long to pinch-hit for Boyer. The third baseman was livid as he went back to the clubhouse. Long flew out and Bobby Richardson lined into a doubleplay to end the inning in a game the Yankees would go on to lose.

When Ralph Houk took over as the manager in 1961, Boyer felt a renewed enthusiasm. The Missouri native had a career batting average of .242; his glove, not his bat, was keeping him in the lineup. Boyer hit only .224 in 1961, but as long as he played solid defense Houk would keep penciling his name into the lineup. Yet as good a fielder as Boyer was, he never won a Gold Glove. Boyer became a victim of fate as Baltimore Orioles third baseman and Hall of Famer Brooks Robinson captured the award for 16 straight seasons.

In the 1964 World Series, Clete was matched up against his older brother, Ken Boyer, who was the third baseman for the National League Champion St. Louis Cardinals. Ken hit a grand slam in Game 4 to give the Cardinals a 4–3 win that evened the Series at two games apiece. In Game 7, the Boyer family had reason to be proud. The brothers became the first to each hit a home run in the same World Series game. After the 1966 season, Clete Boyer was traded to the Atlanta Braves where he replaced Hall of Fame third baseman Eddie Matthews.

29. In August of 1968 the Yankees faced a brutal stretch of games, playing three doubleheaders in three days.

Two days before, in the second game of a doubleheader, the Yankees played a 19-inning, 3–3 tie with the Detroit Tigers, so their pitching staff was already overworked. In Game 1 of the first of the three twin bills, the Yankees trailed the Tigers, 4–0. Outfielder Rocky Colavito, who was known for having a strong arm, relieved Yankees starting pitcher Steve Barber in the fourth inning with two men on base and one out. Colavito did not start the game in the outfield, so he had a chance to warm up in the bullpen for this rare appearance. (The outfielder had previously pitched for the Cleveland Indians in 1958.) The Bronx native set down Hall of Famer Al Kaline and Willie Horton, and then pitched two more scoreless innings. The Yankees rallied to win and Colavito was the winning pitcher. In the second game, Colavito hit a home run and the Yankees swept both games.

The next day, in Game 2, shortstop Gene "Stick" Michael pitched three innings in a 10–2 loss to the California Angels. Michael, who did not start, relieved starting pitcher Al Downing to start the seventh inning. He did not walk a batter and had three strikeouts, but gave up five unearned runs in his only game as a pitcher.

Colavito had always wanted to play for his hometown Yankees. He had a "rocket of an arm" that enabled him to make a number of jaw dropping throws to nail base runners trying to advance. Colavito played in only 39 games for the Yankees and was released following the 1968 season.

Michael was the Yankees' starting shortstop from 1969 to 1973. The 6'2" native of Kent, Ohio, went on to manage the Yankees in two separate tenures during the 1981 and 1982 seasons. He became the club's general manager in 1990 and held that position through 1995. Michael is credited with having produced the nucleus of the Yankees championship teams in 1996 and 1998–2000.

30. Right-handed pitcher Vic Raschi was the first Yankee to wear number 42.

Raschi was born in Springfield, Massachusetts, which prompted his nickname, "the Springfield Rifle," for the speed of his fastball. He made his major league debut in late September of 1946. A crowd of 2,475 at Yankee Stadium saw the 27-year-old toss a complete game to beat the Philadelphia Athletics, 9–6, for his first major league win. During the Yankees' run of five straight World Series titles from 1949 to 1953, Raschi had a record of 92–40.

Raschi started the final game of the 1949 season against the Boston Red Sox at Yankee Stadium. The teams were tied for first place; this was a do or die game to decide the American League pennant. The Yankees right-hander pitched eight scoreless innings, but gave up three runs in the ninth. With the tying run at the plate, Raschi got Red Sox catcher Birdie Tebbetts to foul out to first baseman Tommy Henrich for the victory. Off the mound, the right-hander was shy and reserved, but on the hill he was a fiery competitor who sparkled in big games. Raschi was 5–3 in World Series play. In two of the three losses, he went eight innings and twice gave up only one earned run.

In Game 1 of the 1950 World Series, Raschi was brilliant as he led the Yankees to a 1–0 win over the Philadelphia Phillies at Shibe Park. The "Springfield Rifle" gave up two hits, both in the fifth inning, and set down the final nine Phillies hitters. In 1953, Raschi signed a contract for $40,000 and won 13 games. Yankee general manager George Weiss considered that a "down year" for the pitcher and wanted to cut Raschi's contract by a reported 25%.

In 1954, Raschi refused to sign a contract and held out until spring training. When he got to St. Petersburg, Florida (the Yankees' training camp site), he was told by newspaper reporters, not Weiss, that he had been sold to the St. Louis Cardinals.

3

MVP LEVEL

(Answers begin on page 99.)

Now we're getting serious.

Good job getting past the All-Star Level, but you really have to lift your game if you want to consider yourself an MVP.

1. David Wells and David Cone pitched perfect games at Yankee Stadium during the 1998 and 1999 seasons, respectively. With one out in the eighth inning of both games, the same player made a key defensive play to preserve the gems. Name him.

2. On June 28, 2009, Mariano Rivera recorded his 500th save against the New York Mets at Citi Field. In that same game, Rivera did two things he had never done in his entire career. Name those two personal accomplishments. For a bonus: Which pitcher replaced Rivera in the final game of his career?

3. I played with the Yankees for 10 of my 11 major league seasons. I made my major league debut a year after the Yankees dynasty ended. My claim to fame is that I am one of two players to break up three no-hit bids in the ninth inning. Who am I?

4. When the Yankees acquired outfielder Paul O'Neill from the Cincinnati Reds in 1992, whom did they send back to complete the trade?

5. Who holds the Yankees franchise record for most walks drawn in one season by a right-handed hitter?

6. Two players have hit walkoff pennant-winning home runs in Yankees franchise history. Name them.

7. How many Yankees have been named the World Series Most Valuable Player?

8. What position did Thurman Munson play in his final game?

9. Name the Yankees pitcher who came out of retirement to pitch in the 1968 Mayor's Trophy Game against the New York Mets.

10. In 1961, the Yankees carried three catchers on their roster who each hit 20 or more home runs that season. Hall of Famer Yogi Berra and Elston Howard were two of that trio. Who was the third catcher?

11. Match 'Em Up . . . Match each of the following players with what he did in the final game at the original Yankee Stadium:

Last Yankees hit	Jose Molina
Last Yankee to score a run	Cody Ransom
Last Yankees RBI	Jason Giambi
Last Yankees home run	Derek Jeter
Last Yankee to bat	Brett Gardner
Last Yankees strikeout by pitcher	Andy Pettitte
Last Yankee to make an error	Joba Chamberlain
Last Yankees putout	Robinson Cano

12. In the history of the franchise, three players have each had six hits in a single game. Name them.

13. Hall of Famer Whitey Ford is one of two Yankee pitchers to have won a Cy Young Award and a World Series Most Valuable Player Award in the same season. Name the other Yankee to accomplish this feat.

14. During his record-setting season of 1961, Roger Maris hit 61 home runs. How many times was he intentionally walked?

15. In 1985, Yankees first baseman Don Mattingly drove in 145 runs. Leadoff batter Rickey Henderson scored 146 runs. How many times did Henderson score when

Mattingly was at bat? Bonus: How many runs did Henderson score on a Mattingly home run?

16. Name the starting eight for the 1927 Yankees.

17. On June 20, 1963, the Yankees beat the Washington Senators, 5–4, on a walkoff hit by Bobby Richardson in the bottom of the ninth at Yankee Stadium. Besides winning the game, what was the significance of that day in Yankees history?

18. Name the eight Yankees who have hit walkoff grand slam home runs.

19. Can you name the Yankees lineup that took the field when the infamous "pine tar game" resumed in August of 1983?

20. Name the seven Yankees who hit .400 or better in multiple World Series.

MVP-LEVEL ANSWERS

1. Chuck Knoblauch was the Yankees second baseman who made both defensive plays that saved the perfect games thrown by David Wells in 1998 and David Cone in 1999.

On May 17, 1998, Yankees left-hander David Wells retired the first 22 Minnesota Twins hitters. With one out in the eighth, Twins first baseman Ron Coomer hit a hard ground-ball to the right of Yankees second baseman Chuck Knoblauch. It appeared as if Coomer would become the first Minnesota player to reach base, but Knoblauch knocked the ball down and, after it rolled a little to his right, he picked it up and threw out the runner to preserve the perfect game.

Fourteen months later, it was like (as Yogi Berra coined the phrase) "déjà vu all over again." David Cone set down the first 22 Montreal Expos hitters. With one out in the eighth, Expos second baseman Jose Vidro hit a grounder towards the middle that seemed destined to get past the infield. Knoblauch moved quickly to his right and was able to backhand the ball. He then steadied himself to make the throw and get the out. Ironically, the same spot in the batting order created the key defensive play to the same defender to preserve both perfect games.

Knoblauch began his career with the Twins and was the 1991 American League Rookie of the Year. Right before spring training began in 1998, the Yankees acquired Knoblauch from the Twins in a four-for-one swap. The Houston, Texas, native played on three championship teams in four seasons with the Yankees.

Yankees owner George Steinbrenner was always infatuated with the idea of putting Wells in pinstripes. After the 1996 season, the 33-year-old became a free agent and Steinbrenner seized the opportunity to sign the left-hander. Wells had an outstanding first year in New York. The portly southpaw tossed 218 innings and was 16–10.

In 1998, Wells was 18–8 and became the nominal ace of the staff on a team that won 114 regular season games. Wells went 4–0 in the postseason to lead the Yankees to their 24th World Series title. In February of 1999, Wells was traded to the Toronto Blue Jays as part of a four-player swap for Roger Clemens.

During his four-year tenure with the Yankees (which included a second stint in 2002 and 2003), the left-hander was 68–28 for a .708 winning percentage, and a 3.90 earned run average. In postseason play as a Yankee, Wells won seven of 10 decisions.

In July of 1995, the Yankees were right in the thick of the race for the initial American League wild card spot. Management felt the team needed one more starting pitcher. On July 28th, the Yankees acquired former Cy Young Award winner David Cone from the Toronto Blue Jays for three minor league prospects. The right-hander was among the top pitchers in baseball, and his experience in postseason and World Series play was invaluable to a team that was learning how to win.

Cone made 13 starts for the Yankees, and was 9–2 down the stretch to help the team make the playoffs for the first time in 14 seasons. In May of 1996, Cone was diagnosed with an aneurysm in his right arm and missed four months of the season. He returned on September 2nd to throw seven no-hit innings against the Athletics in Oakland.

Cone started Game 3 of the 1996 World Series against Atlanta and tossed six strong innings in a 5–2 win that many felt helped turn the Series around. In parts of six seasons with the Yankees, Cone compiled a 64–40 record with a .615 winning percentage.

David Cone's postseason experience was key to the Yankees' success in the mid-to-late 90s. (clare-and-ben via Wikimedia Commons)

2. Mariano Rivera, who is baseball's all-time saves leader, recorded his 500th career save against the New York Mets at Citi Field on June 28, 2009.

In that game, Rivera not only drew the first and only base on balls of his career, he also logged his first and only RBI. With two on and two out, and the Yankees holding a one-run lead, Rivera got the final out of the eighth. Since the game was played at a National League ballpark—no designated hitter allowed—Rivera had to be inserted into the batting order. With runners at first and second and two out in the ninth, Derek Jeter was intentionally walked to bring up Rivera. "Mo" had only two previous major league at-bats, with never a hit nor a run batted in. With the bases loaded Rivera faced Mets closer Francisco Rodriguez, who fell behind in the count, 2–0. Rodriguez evened the count at 2–2 with a pair of called strikes. After Rivera fouled off the fifth pitch, Rodriguez threw ball three and then ball four.

A sellout crowd of over 41,000 was on hand, including many Yankees fans. When Rivera began his trot to first, a roar went up from the crowd as they recognized what had just happened. Rivera set down the Mets in the ninth to reach the coveted milestone of 500 saves.

Rivera's first major league at-bat had come in 2006 against the Philadelphia Phillies at Citizens Bank Park; he struck out. The native of Panama was a great athlete who would always shag fly balls in the outfield before games. He hoped to play center field in a major league game one day. In May of 2012, Rivera was doing just that when he tore the ACL (anterior cruciate ligament) in his right knee while chasing a fly ball during batting practice. As he was tracking the ball, Rivera's knee buckled and he crashed into the center field wall. At first some thought he was playfully faking it, but it became clear that Rivera was in excruciating pain. The Yankees closer underwent surgery and vowed to return in the 2013 season.

He came back, and he didn't skip a beat as he recorded 44 saves in his final season.

There was talk before Rivera's final game in late September of 2013 that he would possibly play an inning in center field. Yankees manager Joe Girardi had reportedly considered using Rivera in the field. Many of those around the team thought he may have been the best fielding center fielder on their roster. The Yankees were out of the race, but because of his knee injury two years earlier, Rivera was reluctant to play the outfield.

On September 26, 2013, the Yankees trailed the Tampa Rays, 4–0, in the top of the eighth. With two on and one out, Rivera's signature entrance song, Metallica's "Enter Sandman," played one final time as the Yankees closer was called into the game. The sellout throng of over 48,000 was on their feet to honor one of the best pitchers in franchise history. Rivera got the final two outs of the eighth. In the ninth, Rivera got the first two outs and then was ceremoniously lifted from the game in favor of relief pitcher Matt Daley. Longtime teammates and friends Derek Jeter and Andy Pettitte surprised Rivera by being the ones who came out of the dugout to make the change, a move that was arranged by manager Joe Girardi in cooperation with the umpires.

Rivera was overcome with emotion as he hugged his teammates. Amidst a thunderous standing ovation, he left the field for the final time.

3. In 1965, the Yankees were experiencing the first season of their post-dynasty era.

Following their seven-game loss to the St. Louis Cardinals in the 1964 World Series, the team went through management and ownership changes. Manager Yogi Berra was fired in October. A month later, Dan Topping and Del Webb, the team's co-owners, sold 80 percent interest in the club to CBS. The new owners took over not only an aging team. Attendance was dwindling and the farm system was barren of any future stars. There was some talent in the minors, but not enough to avoid what would become a 12-year championship drought.

In May of 1965, the Yankees would promote a switch-hitting second baseman from their AAA Richmond affiliate who would become symbolic of an era without any World Series titles. Horace Clarke made his major league debut on May 13 at Fenway Park. Clarke was a 5'9" 24-year-old, switch-hitting second baseman who was projected to be the heir apparent to Bobby Richardson, who was to retire following the 1966 season. From 1967 to 1973, Clarke became the everyday second baseman. His best season was 1969, when he batted .285 with 33 stolen bases. The Virgin Islands native hit only 27 home runs in his major league career, but he's the only major leaguer whose first two home runs were grand slams.

Clarke was not a Gold Glove caliber fielder, and his defensive skills came into question as he got older.

Clarke had a reputation for not "hanging in" on the doubleplay. He was accused by some of jumping up to avoid the oncoming runner who was attempting to break up the doubleplay, although he led the league twice in turning doubleplays as a second baseman.

Clarke has a unique distinction in baseball history. Within a one-month span of the 1970 season, he became the first player to break up three no-hit bids in the ninth inning.

(Minnesota Twins catcher Joe Mauer is the only other player to do it.) On June 4th at Yankee Stadium, the Yankees trailed the Kansas City Royals 1–0. Pitcher Jim Rooker took a no-hitter to the bottom of the ninth. Clarke led off the inning with a single to right field to spoil the bid.

A little over two weeks later at Fenway Park, Boston Red Sox pitcher Sonny Siebert was pitching a no-hitter against the Yankees. Once again, Clarke was the leadoff batter in the ninth and he spoiled this bid with a single to center field.

Finally, on July 2 at Detroit's Tiger Stadium, Joe Niekro was no-hitting the Yankees heading to the top of the ninth. After pinch-hitter Pete Ward flied out to center field for the first out, Clarke spoiled his third no-hit bid with an infield single.

In 1973, the Yankees were sold for $10 million to a group headed by George Steinbrenner. The team was going through another transition, and Clarke was heading into the twilight of his career. Yankee Stadium was being renovated, so the team played the 1974 and 1975 seasons at Shea Stadium in Queens, New York. Clarke began the 1974 season on the roster, but Sandy Alomar Sr. took over at second base. In May of that year Clarke was sold to the San Diego Padres, where he played his final major league season.

4. In November of 1992, the Yankees acquired outfielder Paul O'Neill from the Cincinnati Reds in exchange for outfielder Roberto Kelly.

The native of Panama was being projected as a "five-tool" player who could hit, hit with power, field his position, throw, and run. Following the 1992 season, Kelly was 28 years old and was heading into his prime, but the Yankees felt he had reached his peak and that his right-handed bat would not play well at Yankee Stadium as he got older.

O'Neill, who had won a World Series ring with the Reds in 1990, was a fierce competitor who wore his emotions on his sleeve. The rap on the 29-year-old left-hand hitting outfielder was that he could not hit left-handed pitching. As an added bonus, O'Neill was a solid defensive right fielder who possessed a good arm.

Yankees general manager Gene Michael felt that Kelly was productive but undisciplined at the plate. At the time, the Yankees were trying to be a team that was patient at the plate and got on base.

The Columbus, Ohio, native won over the New York fans with his intense desire to win. That desire would inspire George Steinbrenner to coin O'Neill's moniker, "The Warrior."

After the Yankees opened the 1993 season with a five-game road trip, O'Neill was hitting .316 with a home run and five runs batted in. The script couldn't have been written any better for the 30-year-old in his home debut against Kansas City. O'Neill was 4-for-4 with a double and a triple, and two RBIs, to lead the Yankees to a 4–1 win. O'Neill completed his first season with 20 home runs and 75 RBIs while hitting .311.

His second year was the strike-shortened season of 1994, but it was O'Neill's best individual campaign with the Yankees. O'Neill won the American League batting title with a .359 average, and finished fifth in the voting for the Most Valuable Player Award. In each of his first six seasons with the Yankees, O'Neill batted .300 or better.

Baseball expanded its playoff format in 1995, with the creation of three divisions and the addition of one wild card team in each league. A labor dispute shortened the season to

144 games. With 31 games remaining to play, the Yankees were 54–59 and did not seem as though they would snap their postseason drought, which now stood at 14 seasons. In the finale of a three-game series sweep over the California Angels, O'Neill was 4-for-4 with a career-high three home runs and eight runs batted in. O'Neill hit in 23 of the team's final 31 games as the Yankees captured the first American League Wild Card berth. O'Neill acquitted himself well in the ALDS loss to Seattle, hitting in four of the five games and driving in six runs.

In Game 5 of the 1996 World Series, the Yankees led the Atlanta Braves, 1–0. With two out in the bottom of the ninth, Atlanta had the tying run at third and the winning run at first. Yankees closer John Wetteland faced pinch-hitter and former Yankee Luis Polonia. On an 0–2 pitch, Polonia sent a drive toward the right-center field gap. O'Neill, who was playing with an injured hamstring, went back and reached up with his glove to snare the ball and end the game.

O'Neill was an integral part of three more Yankees championship teams. Game 5 of the 2001 World Series turned out to be O'Neill's final home game as a Yankee. Even though he had not yet made it official, the fans sensed he would retire after the season and started to chant his name in the ninth inning. O'Neill had the unique distinction of playing in three perfect games: one with the Reds (Tom Browning in 1988) and two (David Wells in 1998, David Cone in 1999) with the Yankees.

5. Willie Randolph was not known for his power, but he had a great eye at the plate that gave him the ability to draw walks.

In 1980, Randolph led the American League, and set the Yankees' franchise record for a right-handed hitter as he drew

119 walks. His on-base percentage of .427 was second in the league to Hall of Famer George Brett.

On December 11, 1975, the Yankees acquired Randolph, along with pitchers Ken Brett (George Brett's brother) and Dock Ellis from Pittsburgh in exchange for right-handed pitcher George "Doc" Medich. The 1972 seventh-round pick of the Pirates grew up in Brooklyn, New York, where he attended Tilden High School. The 21-year-old won the James P. Dawson Award as the outstanding Yankees rookie in spring training in 1976, but he got off to a slow start when the season began. The first-year Yankee did not get a hit in any of his first three games, but he finally broke out with two hits, including a solo home run, off Baltimore Orioles pitcher and Hall of Famer Jim Palmer.

In April, Randolph helped christen the revamped Yankee Stadium with two hits, two runs scored, and an RBI as the Yankees beat the Minnesota Twins, 11–4. With Randolph as their starting second baseman, the Yankees won their first ever American League East Division title, and the American League pennant for the first time in 12 years. The Yankees repeated, winning the American League East division title in 1977, and for a second straight season they faced the Kansas City Royals in the best-of-five championship series.

The Yankees were trailing, 3–1, in the eighth inning of the decisive Game 5 in Kansas City. Randolph singled to lead off the inning and eventually scored the second run. The Yankees rallied for three more runs in the ninth. Randolph drove in the go-ahead run with a sacrifice fly and was part of executing a game-ending doubleplay in the field. The Yankees went on to a thrilling 5–3 win to clinch their second consecutive American League pennant.

In Game 1 of the World Series against the Los Angeles Dodgers, Randolph doubled and scored the winning run in the bottom of the 12th on Paul Blair's walkoff RBI single. Randolph played a major role in the Yankees' historic comeback against the Boston Red Sox in 1978. The Yankees rallied to cut down a double-digit deficit in July to only four games as the two teams opened a four-game series in early September at Fenway Park. Randolph was 8-for-16 with five runs scored and six runs batted in as the Yankees swept four games from Boston in what has become known as "the Boston Massacre," to pull into a tie for first in the American League East with 20 games to play.

But the Yankees' second baseman suffered a tough break with just three days left in the regular season. Randolph injured his hamstring running to first and was out for the rest of the season. He would go on to miss the one-game playoff victory against Boston and the entire postseason. Randolph's numbers in the 1980 season earned him the first Silver Slugger Award for American League second basemen. He played 13 seasons with the Yankees, was a six-time All-Star, holds the franchise record for games played at second base with 1,689, and is honored with a plaque in Monument Park at Yankee Stadium.

6. Chris Chambliss and Aaron Boone are the two Yankees who have hit walkoff pennant-winning home runs.

The two historic blasts had some similarities. Both came in an "all or nothing" final game of an American League Championship Series. On October 14, 1976, the Yankees and Royals were tied heading to the bottom of the ninth of a fifth and deciding game of the ALCS at Yankee Stadium. On October

16, 2003, the Yankees and Red Sox were tied heading to the bottom of the 11th in a seventh and deciding game of the ALCS at Yankee Stadium. (The ALCS had expanded to a best of seven in 1985.) Chambliss and Boone both led off their respective innings. There was a slight delay before Chambliss would take his position in the batter's box. Royals reliever Mark Littell, who was pitching in his third inning of work, took a few extra warm-ups as the field was being cleared from the debris that was thrown by the raucous and prematurely celebrating fans. Littell threw a first pitch fastball and Chambliss slammed it over the right-center field wall to send the Yankees back to the World Series for the first time since 1964.

Chambliss had been selected first overall by the Cleveland Indians in the 1970 amateur draft. The 6'1", 195-pound first baseman was named the American League's Rookie of the Year in 1971. Nearly a month into the 1974 season, Chambliss was traded to the Yankees as part of a controversial seven-player deal. In that trade, the Yankees dealt four pitchers to Cleveland for Chambliss and pitchers Cecil Upshaw and Dick Tidrow, who turned into a reliable relief pitcher in the championship seasons of 1977 and 1978.

The Yankees loved Chambliss's left-handed bat at Yankee Stadium, so they felt the price was worth it. Chambliss gave Yankees fans a moment during the regular season that was a portent of things to come later in the year. The Yankees hosted the Boston Red Sox in late July, but the teams were on opposite sides of the standings spectrum. The Yankees led the American League East with a 59–33 record, while Boston was in last place with a 42–50 mark.

No matter, it was still the Yankees vs. the Red Sox, so the game did not lack for intensity. Boston had a 5–0 lead, but the

Yankees chipped away and made it a 5–3 deficit entering the last of the ninth. The hulking first baseman hit a three-run, walkoff home run into the right-center field bleachers that gave the Yankees a 6–5 victory.

Chambliss played with the Yankees from 1974 to 1979, and one game in 1988. In November of 1979 Chambliss was traded to Toronto, which shipped him to Atlanta a month later. Twenty-seven years and two days after Chambliss won the American League pennant with a memorable long ball, third baseman Aaron Boone duplicated the feat.

The right-handed hitting Boone blasted his home run off knuckleball pitcher Tim Wakefield into the left field stands, while the left-handed hitting Chambliss had smacked his into the right-center field bullpen area. Like Chambliss, Boone came to the Yankees in a trade with a team based in Ohio. The Yankees beat the July 31st trade deadline by acquiring the third baseman from the Cincinnati Reds. In January of 2004, Boone injured his knee playing pick-up basketball. Boone's player contract was voided because of a stipulation that he was not allowed to play basketball. That injury led the Yankees to pursue a trade with Texas for Alex Rodriguez; Boone was released in March of 2004.

7. The World Series Most Valuable Player Award was instituted in 1955, when Brooklyn Dodgers pitcher Johnny Podres copped the initial award.

Since that time, the honor has been bestowed on 12 Yankees. In 1956, pitcher Don Larsen tossed the first perfect game in World Series history and became the first Yankees winner. A 17-player trade with the Baltimore Orioles in 1954 had brought Larsen and pitcher Bob Turley to the Yankees. That swap looked even better when Turley won the World Series MVP in 1958. The right-hander keyed the Yankees' comeback from a 3–1 Series deficit against the Milwaukee Braves. For the only time in history, a member of the losing team was named the World Series MVP Award winner; he was also the third Yankee to be so honored.

Second baseman Bobby Richardson had such an outstanding Series (.367, Series record 12 RBIs) against the Pittsburgh Pirates that he still captured the award despite the team losing in seven games.

The following season, Hall of Famer Whitey Ford won the award. Ford was 2–0 in the 1961 World Series. The Yankee left-hander tossed a complete game, two-hit shutout in Game 1. Ford also broke Babe Ruth's World Series record of 29 2/3 scoreless innings. Ford extended the streak to 33 2/3 innings, which is still a record to this day. (Note: Mariano Rivera set the postseason record in 2000.)

Ralph Terry, who gave up Mazeroski's famous home run in 1960, got his revenge in 1962 when he led the Yankees to a seven-game victory over the San Francisco Giants. Terry tossed a complete game, four-hit shutout as the Yankees won the Series with a thrilling 1–0 win in Game 7. Fifteen years would go by before another Yankee would win the award. Reggie Jackson left no doubts when he captured MVP honors in 1977. Jackson became the second player to hit three home runs in a World Series game when he achieved the feat in the clinching Game 6. The controversial slugger hit a total of five home runs in the Series and won his second MVP. (Jackson had won the award with the Oakland A's in 1973.)

In 1978, shortstop Bucky Dent hit one of the most famous home runs in Yankees history to beat the Boston Red

Sox in a one-game playoff for the American League's Eastern Division title. Dent continued his surprising offensive output in the 1978 World Series, hitting .417 with 10 runs batted in, to lead the Yankees to their 22nd world championship.

Closer John Wetteland became the eighth Yankee to capture the award in 1996. Wetteland had four saves in five appearances as the Yankees won their first World Series in 18 years.

Third baseman Scott Brosius made the most of his first World Series. Brosius hit .417 in the four-game sweep of the San Diego Padres, with two home runs and six runs batted in.

The Yankees made it back-to-back titles with a four-game sweep of the Atlanta Braves in 1999. There was no clear winner, but closer Mariano Rivera won the award as he won one game and saved two others.

In 2000, Derek Jeter became the only player to win the World Series MVP Award and the All-Star MVP award in the same season. Jeter hit .409 in the 2002 World Series against the crosstown rival New York Mets. After the Mets had won Game 3 to narrow the Yankees' Series lead to two games to one, the Yankees' captain led off Game 4 with a home run that took back the momentum. The Yankees went on to win the Series in five games.

Hideki Matsui became the first Japanese native to win the award when he batted .615 in the 2009 World Series win against the Philadelphia Phillies. Matsui tied Richardson's Series record in the clinching Game 6 with six runs batted in.

8. A day before he died in a tragic plane crash in his hometown of Canton, Ohio, Thurman Munson started at first base against the Chicago White Sox at Comiskey Park.

It was his third straight start at the position, and only the fifth time in his career that he ever started at first base. After he struck out in the top of the third, Jim Spencer replaced Munson. Little did anyone know at the time it would be his final game. The 32-year-old was bruised and battered from all his years behind the plate. The Yankees were using him in different positions to take some pressure off his tired body. Munson's last game as a catcher was July 27th in Milwaukee. The Yankees captain had earned a pilot's license and owned his own plane, so he was able to fly home on off days in the latter stages of his career.

With the fourth overall pick of the 1968 amateur draft, the Yankees had selected Munson. The Canton, Ohio, native joined the team in September of 1969, and in 1970 he won the starting catching job in spring training. Munson hit .302 in his rookie season and garnered 23 of a possible 24 votes to be named the American League's Rookie of the Year.

Munson had a long-running feud with Boston Red Sox catcher Carlton Fisk. It came to a head in August of 1973 in a game at Fenway Park. In the top of the ninth of a tie game, Munson tried to score from third on a failed suicide squeeze bunt attempt by Yankee shortstop Gene Michael. Munson barreled into the Red Sox catcher at the plate, but Fisk held on to the ball to get the out. The Yankees catcher tried to keep Fisk down to allow Felipe Alou, who was also on base, to keep running. Punches were exchanged and Fisk had Michael on the ground as Red Sox pitcher John Curtis grabbed Munson.

Munson was known as a clutch-hitter. In 1975 and 1976, he put together back-to-back 100 RBI seasons. Munson became the third catcher (Yogi Berra, Elston Howard) in franchise history to be named the American League's Most Valuable Player, in 1976. He drew national attention in the 1976 World Series against the Cincinnati Reds. The Yankees were swept in four games, but Munson was a one man show as he batted an amazing .529.

After Reggie Jackson signed a free agent contract to join the Yankees in 1977, some controversial comments about the Yankees catcher/captain surfaced in an issue of *Sport Magazine.* In referring to his joining the Yankees, Jackson was quoted as saying, "I'm the straw that stirs the drink, Munson can only stir it bad." That didn't sit well with Munson nor his teammates, who were fully behind their captain.

Despite a controversial and eventful 1977 season, Munson and Jackson were the forces that drove the Yankees to their first World Series in fifteen years. The 1978 campaign would be Munson's final full season behind the plate.

The Yankees staged their great comeback and beat Boston in a one-game playoff to win the American League East division title. Munson contributed an RBI double to one of the great wins in Yankees history.

In the best-of-five American League Championship Series, the battered backstop overcame a sore shoulder to hit a memorable home run to win Game 3. The series was tied at a game apiece, and the Royals had taken a 5–4 lead in the top of the eighth. On a 2–0 pitch from Royals reliever Doug Bird, Munson hit a long drive that carried just to the left of the 430-foot sign and into the stands in left-center field for a two-run home run. The Yankees won Game 3, and then took the Series in four games before going on to win their second consecutive World Series.

The loss of their captain in 1979 sapped the heart and soul from the team. Two days after his death, the Yankees officially retired Munson's number 15. His empty locker remained in the Yankee clubhouse, never to be used again.

9. Yankees left-hander Whitey Ford pitched his last game on May 21, 1967, at Detroit's Tiger Stadium.

The Hall of Famer started and lasted only one inning. Ford's arm troubles had gotten the best of him. Nine days after that fateful start, he officially announced his retirement. A little over a year later, Whitey Ford was back on the mound attempting a comeback in the annual "Mayor's Trophy Game" against the crosstown New York Mets at Shea Stadium. In the bottom of the sixth, Ford struck out Mets third baseman Ed Charles and then got center fielder Tommie Agee and left fielder Don Bosch on groundouts.

He also found himself in a little controversy: Home plate umpire Ken Burkhart called two automatic balls against Ford for going to his mouth. It would be his final appearance on a major league pitching mound.

Whitey Ford is considered by many to be the greatest pitcher in Yankees franchise history. During his 16-year career, the New York–born and bred left-hander helped lead the Yankees to 11 American League pennants and six world championships. Ford's arm first caught the eye of a scout at a tryout at Yankee Stadium in 1946. Midway through the 1950 season, the Yankees promoted Ford from their AAA affiliate in Kansas City. In July of that year, Ford got his first major league win when he beat the Chicago White Sox. The southpaw started to blossom, giving up only one run in each of three consecutive complete game wins in August.

With 15 games left in the season, the Yankees trailed the Detroit Tigers by a half game for first place in the American

League when the teams met at Detroit's Briggs Stadium. Yankees manager Casey Stengel gave the ball to his young lefthander, who delivered a complete game win that brought his record to 7–0. The Yankees took over first place and never looked back. With a three games to none lead in the World Series vs. Philadelphia, Ford came within an out of going the distance in Game 4 as the Yankees swept the Phillies.

The southpaw was the focal point of some second-guessing of Stengel in the 1960 World Series loss to the Pittsburgh Pirates. The Yankees manager held Ford out until Game 3 at Yankee Stadium. It was reported that Stengel felt the hard infield at Forbes Field, and the Pirates offense—which was predominantly right-handed—was not a good combination for Ford, who was a left-handed groundball pitcher. Ford pitched complete game shutouts in Games 3 and 6, but was not available for the crushing defeat in Game 7. After the Series was over, Stengel was roundly criticized. Five days later, he was fired and replaced by Ralph Houk.

Ford's best season was 1961, when he won the Cy Young Award with a 25–4 record. Three of the four losses were by scores of 1–0, 2–1, and 2–1.

In the World Series against Cincinnati, Ford blanked the Reds with a complete game two-hitter. He was named the Series MVP. That gave Ford 27 consecutive scoreless innings in World Series play, just shy of Babe Ruth's Series record of 29 2/3 scoreless innings. In Game 4, Ford added five more shutout innings to break Ruth's record, but had to leave the game after he fouled a ball off his foot.

The lefty faced the San Francisco Giants in Game 1 of the 1962 World Series, and added an inning and two-thirds to his record total that reached 33 2/3 scoreless innings. In his final two seasons, Ford began experiencing arm trouble and won a total of only four games. In the early stages of his final season of 1967, Ford looked as though he could still be a consistent winner, but arm trouble plagued him. The southpaw was dealing with painful bone spurs in his elbow, which motivated him to announce his retirement. Ford finished with a franchise-leading 236 victories and a .690 winning percentage that earns him a tie for third on baseball's all-time list.

10. In 1961, three Yankees catchers hit more than 20 home runs.

Elston Howard, who was the starting catcher, hit 21 home runs. Yogi Berra, who was then 36 years old, was starting in left field and was the third catcher. The three-time American League Most Valuable Player slammed 22 home runs. The other catcher was Johnny Blanchard, nicknamed "Super Sub," who delivered 21 home runs as part of a Yankees team that hit a record-setting total of 240 round-trippers in 1961.

Blanchard never had his number retired, as did Berra and Howard, but he did grab the spotlight over a three-day period in the middle of the season. On July 21st, the Yankees were trailing the Boston Red Sox, 8–7, in the top of the ninth and had the bases loaded with two out. Yankees manager Ralph Houk sent Blanchard up to bat for Clete Boyer, and he pinch-hit a grand slam to cap off a five-run rally for an 11–8 come-from-behind win.

The next day it was, as "Yogi" used to say, "déjà vu all over again."

In the ninth, the Yankees trailed by a run. Houk used Blanchard again as a pinch-hitter for Boyer and the 28-year-old catcher went deep again. This time, he tied the game and the Yankees went on to win, 11–9.

In their very next game, Blanchard started behind the plate as the Yankees hosted the Chicago White Sox. In the bottom of the first, Mantle and Blanchard hit back-to-back home runs. The Yankee backstop had hit three home runs in his last three at-bats. In his next plate appearance, Blanchard homered again to make it four consecutive at-bats. He also tied a major league record with four home runs in three games. The streak ended when he flied out to the wall in deep right field in his succeeding at-bat. Blanchard set a franchise record with four pinch-hit home runs in 1961.

The heroics didn't stop there. In early August, Blanchard slammed a three-run, walkoff home run in the bottom of the 10th inning off Minnesota Twins left-hander Bill Pleis. The Yankees were locked in a tight pennant race with Detroit; the win gave them a game and a half lead in the American League.

Two days later, the Twins led the Yankees, 6–5, going to the bottom of the 10th. Blanchard led off the inning against Pleis and tied the game with a home run into the right field seats. The Yankees went on to win the game in 15 innings. In Game 3 of the 1961 World Series, the Yankees trailed the Cincinnati Reds, 2–1, in the top of the eighth. Blanchard picked up where he had left off in the regular season by hitting a pinch-hit home run to tie the game. In the Series-clinching Game 5, the left-handed hitting catcher got things going with a two-run home run in the top of the first.

In 1964, Blanchard's home run totals began to drop off and he hit only seven that year. On May 3, 1965, Blanchard was traded to the Kansas City Athletics. Blanchard was devastated. Some of his teammates told reporters he was so distraught that he began crying by his locker.

11. On September 21, 2008, the Yankees hosted the Baltimore Orioles in the final game at Yankee Stadium I.

The last game produced a number of "last" trivia answers beginning with the last hit. In the seventh inning, Yankees first baseman Jason Giambi got the last hit, an RBI single to left field. In December of 2001, the Yankees had signed Giambi to a seven-year, $120 million contract. His signature moment with the Yankees came on May 17, 2002, when he hit a 12th inning, walkoff grand slam to beat the Minnesota Twins, 13–12.

Following the final Stadium hit, outfielder Brett Gardner pinch-ran for Giambi and scored the final run in the history of the ballpark. The 5'11", 195-pound Gardner came up in 2008 and added a dimension of speed to the Yankee lineup. In 2011, he tied for the American League lead with 49 stolen bases. Gardner won a Gold Glove in the 2016 season.

The final run at the stadium scored on the final run batted in. Robinson Cano's RBI single capped the scoring in a 7–3 Yankee win. Cano was promoted in early May of 2005 and immediately assumed the everyday job at second base. In his first season, Cano hit .297, with 14 home runs and 62 RBIs. He finished second in the voting for American League Rookie of the Year, losing out to Oakland A's closer Huston Street. Cano's best overall season with the Yankees was 2010, when he hit .319 with 29 home runs, 109 runs batted in, and a .914 OPS. Cano was a steady presence in the everyday lineup from 2005 to 2013. During his nine-year Yankee career, Cano hit for a .309 average, with 204 home runs and 822 RBIs.

The final home run at the stadium came off the bat of someone who had hit fewer than 40 home runs in his entire major league career. Center fielder Johnny Damon homered in the third inning with what appeared at the time might be the final home run.

One inning later, backup catcher Jose Molina hit a two-run home run off Orioles starting pitcher Chris Waters for what proved to be the last home run at the stadium. The veteran backup catcher had a great game in the Stadium finale, with three hits and two runs scored.

The Yankees' final at-bat came in the bottom of the 8th inning. Molina lined out to right field, Damon fouled out to the shortstop and, in the final Yankee at-bat, Derek Jeter grounded out to third.

After the game, Jeter authored a poignant moment when he addressed the crowd of 54,610: "We're relying on you to take the memories from this stadium and add them to the new memories that come to the new Yankee Stadium, and continue to pass them on from generation to generation. On behalf of this entire organization, we want to take this moment to salute you, the greatest fans in the world."

Relief pitcher Joba Chamberlain recorded the final strikeout when he got the Orioles' designated hitter, Aubrey Huff, swinging in the top of the seventh. Chamberlain had debuted in relief on August 7, 2007, pitching two scoreless innings in a win at Toronto. He did not give up an earned run in his first 12 appearances spanning the first 17 innings pitched in his major league career. In June of 2011, he underwent "Tommy John" surgery. Then, in March of 2012, Chamberlain suffered an ankle injury that left him spewing blood. He did not return until August and played one more season with the Yankees. Starting pitcher Andy Pettitte committed the last Yankees error in the third inning. Pettitte bobbled a slow groundball in front of home plate that allowed Orioles second baseman Brian Roberts to reach first. The final error in the stadium's history was committed by Orioles shortstop Brandon Fahey in the bottom of the seventh. Mariano Rivera threw the last pitch to Roberts, who hit a grounder toward the right side. First baseman Cody Ransom fielded it and ran to the base for the unassisted, and final, putout in Yankee Stadium history.

12. The three players who each have had a six-hit game in Yankees franchise history are outfielder Myril Hoag, outfielder Gerald Williams, and outfielder Johnny Damon.

In the first game of a doubleheader at Fenway Park on June 6, 1934, the Sacramento native Hoag tied an American League record with six singles in six at-bats as the Yankees walloped the Red Sox, 15–3. Hoag singled in the second, third, fourth, and fifth innings. He did not bat in the sixth, but got his fifth single in the seventh inning as the Yankees were blowing the game open. Hoag's final hit came in the top of the eighth when he singled to left field, but Lou Gehrig was thrown out at home to end the inning.

It would take 62 years and a 15-inning game for another Yankee to have six hits in a single game.

On May 1, 1996, the Yankees beat the Orioles 11–6 in 15 innings at Camden Yards. Left fielder Gerald Williams had six hits in eight at-bats to tie the franchise record for hits in a single game, although it was in extra innings. Williams's memorable day began with a two-run home run in the second. He singled in the fourth, flied out in the sixth, and singled again in the eighth. Williams had three hits and the Yankees had a one-run lead heading to the bottom of the ninth. The Orioles tied the game, sending it into extra innings and giving Williams some additional at-bats. The Yankees outfielder singled in the 11th and 12th innings, but the game continued. His final hit came in a five-run rally in the top of the 15th, when he singled in a run to cap off the scoring. Williams played parts of seven seasons with the Yankees. Johnny Damon's six-hit game came in nine innings, but it was the most memorable of the three because of the way the game ended.

On June 7, 2008, the Yankees were trailing the Kansas City Royals, 10–8, in the bottom of the eighth. Damon already had four straight hits when he faced Royals pitcher Ramon Ramirez with runners at second and third and one out. Damon's fifth hit was a line single to left that scored both runs to tie the game at 10. In the top of the ninth, Royals outfielder David DeJesus hit a solo home run off Mariano Rivera to give Kansas City an 11–10 lead. Jorge Posada's solo home run with one out in the bottom of the ninth tied the game at 11. With two out and no one on, Wilson Betemit drew a walk and Melky Cabrera singled to put the winning run on second. Damon came up and stroked a 3–1 pitch from Royals pitcher Joakim Soria to right field to score Betemit with the winning run. The walkoff hit capped off a story book day for the veteran outfielder who went 6-for-6 in the Yankees' win.

But Damon's greatest Yankees moment came in Game 4 of the 2009 World Series against the Philadelphia Phillies. The Phils had just tied the game at 4 in the bottom of the eighth on a solo home run by Pedro Feliz. In the top of the ninth, Damon singled with two out to conclude a nine-pitch duel with Phillies reliever Brad Lidge. With Mark Teixeira due up, the Phillies put on a shift. Shortstop Jimmy Rollins moved to the right of second base, while third baseman Feliz moved over to the vacant shortstop spot. On the first pitch, Damon stole second. Feliz covered the bag, but the throw pulled him off onto the right field side. Damon, who noticed that no one was covering third, bounced right up and took off onto the next 90 feet. Lidge had a "brain lapse" because it was his responsibility to cover third on that play.

Teixeira was hit by a pitch, and Alex Rodriguez doubled to score Damon and give the Yankees a 5–4 lead. The Yankees added two more runs and won the game 7–4 to take a three games to one lead in the Series that they ended in six games. Damon played four of his 18 major league seasons with the Yankees.

13. The only two pitchers in Yankees history to have won a Cy Young Award and a World Series Most Valuable Player Award in the same season were Whitey Ford and Bob Turley.

Ford accomplished the feat in 1961, but Turley was the first to do it, in 1958. "Bullet Bob" threw a blazing fastball with movement that made it very difficult to hit. The right-hander also threw a curveball, changeup and slider, but he "lived" off his fastball. Turley began his major league career with the St. Louis Browns, and moved with the team when it became the Baltimore Orioles in 1954.

Following that season, the Yankees completed a trade with the Orioles that went down as one of the best in team history. As part of a memorable 17-player deal, the Yankees acquired the 23-year-old Turley and 26-year-old right-handed pitcher Don Larsen.

Turley won his first five starts and nearly threw a no-hitter against the Chicago White Sox. He won 17 games in 1955 but took a step backward the next season, winning only eight games in the regular season. In Game 6 of the 1956 World

Series against Brooklyn, Turley pitched into the 10th inning of a 1–0 loss to the Dodgers. He struck out 11 and lost on Jackie Robinson's walkoff, RBI single in the bottom of the 10th. Turley came up big in the 1957 World Series against Milwaukee. With the Yankees facing elimination, the right-hander gave up two runs in a complete game, 3–2 win, which sent the Series to a Game 7. In the top of the ninth, Turley walked Hall of Famer Eddie Mathews, but then struck out Hall of Famer Hank Aaron. Turley ended the game by inducing Wes Covington to hit into a doubleplay. The Braves won the Series, but Turley left an impression that would carry over to the next season.

In 1958, the Troy, Illinois, native captured the Cy Young Award with an American League–leading 21 wins. He also led the major leagues in winning percentage (.750) and tied for the league lead in complete games with 19. The Yankees and Braves met for a second consecutive season in the 1958 World Series. Turley started Game 2 but had a rough time as he lasted only one-third of an inning and gave up four runs. Turley lost Game 2; he started Game 5 and tossed a complete game, five-hit shutout with 10 strikeouts as the Yanks began their comeback from a three games to one deficit. In Game 6, the Yankees scored twice in the top of the 10th to take a 4–2 lead. Milwaukee narrowed the lead to one in the bottom half off Yankees relief pitcher Ryne Duren, and had two men on with two outs. Milwaukee catcher Del Crandall, a right-hand hitter, was due up, but manager Fred Haney went to left-hand hitting pinch-hitter, Frank Torre. Yankees manager Casey Stengel countered with Turley, who was pitching with only one day of rest.

On the first pitch, "Bullet Bob" blew a strike by Torre. The Braves pinch-hitter fouled off the next pitch and then hit a soft line drive to second baseman Gil McDougald, earning Turley the save.

In Game 7, Turley relieved Larsen in the third when the Yankees starter struggled. He allowed a game-tying home run to Crandall in the sixth, but pitched the rest of the way and got the win, as the Yankees took the final game of the Series, 6–2.

Turley was voted the Series MVP. The Yankees avenged the previous year's loss and became only the second team to come from a three games to one Series deficit to win.

In the 1960 World Series against the Pittsburgh Pirates, Turley won Game 2 despite giving up 13 hits. The right-hander started Game 7, but was dealing with bone chips in his elbow and lasted only one-plus inning. Turley's arm was never the same after that; the Yankees sold him to the Los Angeles Angels after the 1962 season.

14. During his record-setting season of 1961, Roger Maris was never intentionally walked.

With Hall of Fame switch-hitter Mickey Mantle hitting behind him, opposing pitchers never wanted to put Maris on base, so they pitched to him. Maris and Mantle staged a classic chase of Babe Ruth's 1927 single-season record of 60 home runs. The two were neck-and-neck throughout the 1961 season, but Mantle suffered an infection in his leg late in the season that put him out of action and cost him his chance to get the record. Baseball commissioner Ford Frick tarnished Maris's pursuit by declaring that the record needed to be set in 154 games, on the basis that the modern season is longer, and that Ruth might have hit more home runs if he had played as many games as today's players.

Beginning with the 1961 season, baseball's regular season had expanded to 162 games. Frick declared that if Maris did not break the mark in 154 games, an asterisk would be placed next to his name in the record books. The notion of an asterisk was a myth that lasted until the early 1990s.

In late August, Maris slammed his 50th home run in the Yankees' 124th game. Ruth did not hit his 50th until the 138th game, so Maris was ahead of the Babe's pace.

Heading into September, Maris needed nine home runs to tie the record. The pressure of breaking Ruth's record according to Frick's declaration was beginning to wear on him mentally and physically. Maris was being terse with the media, and he was losing clumps of his hair from the stress. The schedule also wreaked havoc with Maris's chances of breaking Ruth's mark. In September, Maris had 56 home runs when the Yankees faced a stretch of seven games in six days. Maris failed to homer in any of those seven games. After 149 games, he remained stuck at 56 home runs. Maris ended the drought with his 57th home run on September 16th in Detroit. He hit number 58 the very next day in his 151st game and had three games to tie or break the coveted mark.

In his 154th game of the season, Maris hit his 59th home run in Baltimore off right-hander Milt Pappas in the third inning. In the seventh, Maris nearly tied the record as he drove one deep to right field that hooked foul. Maris hit another long foul in the ninth off Orioles pitcher Hoyt Wilhelm, but his chance to tie ended when he bounced back to the mound. There were still eight games to play.

After Maris went without a home run in the next three games, the Yankees returned home to open the final home stand against the Orioles. Maris tied Ruth's record in the

Roger Maris (l) and Mickey Mantle both chased Babe Ruth's single-season home run record in 1961. (Courtesy of the Boston Public Library, Leslie Jones Collection)

third inning when he drove a 2–2 pitch from Orioles pitcher Jack Fisher that bounced off the upper deck in right field and back onto the field for his 60th home run. As he circled the bases, Maris received a thunderous ovation from the more than 19,000 fans at the Stadium. Maris had two more at-bats to get number 61, but he flied out to right field both times. On October 1, 1961, Roger Maris homered off Boston Red Sox pitcher Tracy Stallard to set a new single-season record. In the bottom of the fourth, Maris hit a 2–0 pitch into the right field stands, just to the side of the Yankees bullpen. The 23,154 fans went crazy as Maris circled the bases. There was a mad scramble in the lower right field stands to retrieve the historic orb. A 19-year-old fan named Sal Durante was sitting in Section 33, Box 163D when he caught the ball.

Maris won his second consecutive American League Most Valuable Player award in 1961. In 1962, Maris finished fifth in the American League with 33 home runs.

In Game 7 of the 1962 World Series against the San Francisco Giants, Maris made a key defensive play in the ninth inning. With two out and Giants pinch-hitter Matty Alou on first, Hall of Famer Willie Mays lined a double into the right field corner. Maris quickly hurried over to cut the ball off to keep Alou from scoring. Willie McCovey followed with a line-out, giving the Yankees the seventh game, 1–0, and the World Series. Following the 1966 season, Maris was traded to the St. Louis Cardinals for infielder Charley Smith. In 1991, an eight-man panel of the Committee for Statistical Accuracy voted unanimously to dismiss the "arbitrary" asterisk next to Maris's name in the record books.

15. Following the 1984 season, the Yankees needed a presence at the top of their lineup.

At the 1984 winter meetings in Houston, the Yankees acquired the best leadoff man in the game when they completed a seven-player trade with the Oakland Athletics for Rickey Henderson.

The Oakland, California, native was not just a stolen base threat. Henderson was a solid hitter who finished second on the all-time list in walks. Henderson was "just what the doctor ordered," as he scored a major league–leading 146 runs in 143 games while leading the American League with 80 stolen bases in 1985. Henderson became the first player since Jimmie Foxx in 1939 to total more runs scored than games played. With 24 home runs, he became the first player in history to achieve 20 homers and 80 stolen bases in a season. Henderson also walked 99 times and finished with a .410 on base percentage.

In 1985, Don Mattingly had a career-high 145 RBIs. Henderson accounted for 56 runs (55 RBIs) while the Yankee first baseman was at bat. (Note: In one of the games, Henderson scored when the opposing pitcher was called for a balk while Mattingly was at bat.)

During the 1985 season, the Yankees were 34–15 when Henderson and Mattingly combined for a run. The duo hooked up for 18 runs in September, when the Yankees were challenging the Toronto Blue Jays for first place in the American League East.

Mattingly hit 12 home runs while Henderson was on base. He had a total of 41 hits that drove in runs with Henderson aboard, including nine doubles and 20 singles. There were six sacrifice flies, six RBI groundouts, and one RBI was credited when Mattingly reached on an error. The best single game was on July 10th, when Mattingly drove in Henderson three times with a pair of sacrifice flies and an RBI double.

The Yankees won 16 of their last 17 in which the combo clicked. Mattingly won the 1985 AL MVP award. Henderson finished third in the voting. With 130 runs scored in 1986, Henderson once again led the major leagues. Henderson stole 87 bases to lead the American League for a seventh consecutive season.

Injuries limited the speedster to 95 games in 1987, and he felt the wrath of Yankees owner George Steinbrenner. In August of 1987, manager Lou Piniella had to clear the air with Henderson. Steinbrenner had issued a written statement

Don Mattingly was the American league MVP in 1985. (RickDikeman via Wikimedia Commons)

saying that Piniella wanted Henderson traded because he was "jaking it" while he was recovering from a pulled hamstring.

In 1988, Henderson bounced back to hit .305, with a major league–leading 93 steals. But the Yankees were heading into a transitory period in 1989, so they traded Henderson, an impending free agent, back to the Oakland Athletics for pitchers Greg Cadaret, Eric Plunk, and outfielder Luis Polonia.

During parts of five seasons with the Yankees, Henderson stole 326 bases to become the franchise's all-time leader, surpassing Hal Chase, who had 248. (Derek Jeter took over the all-time franchise lead in 2011.)

Henderson came under some criticism for what appeared to be a lack of hustle at times, but he is widely regarded as the greatest leadoff hitter of all time.

Henderson broke Lou Brock's all-time record of 938 steals while playing against the Yankees in May of 1991. Henderson, who was inducted into the Baseball Hall of Fame in 2009, set the all-time single-season mark with 130 stolen bases in 1982.

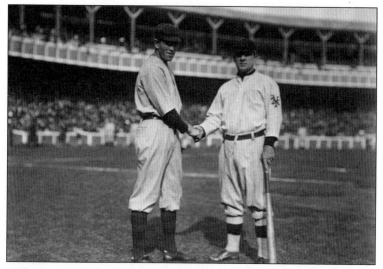

Hal Chase (left, with John McGraw in 1910) held the franchise record for stolen bases until it was broken by Rickey Henderson. (George Grantham Bain Collection, Library of Congress)

16. The 1927 Yankees are regarded by many as the best single-season team in baseball history.

The everyday starting lineup contained four Hall of Famers, including first baseman Lou Gehrig, second baseman Tony

Lazzeri, and outfielders Babe Ruth and Earle Combs. Shortstop Mark Koenig and third baseman Joe Dugan rounded out the infield.

Bob Meusel was the starting left fielder, and Pat Collins caught most of the games. Their first six hitters in the batting order were known as "Murderers' Row" for the way they "murdered" opposing pitchers. Combs led off and had his best season. He batted .356, leading the American League in hits with 231. Koenig was the prototypical number 2 hitter in the order. The 22-year-old from San Francisco, California, struck out only 21 times and scored 99 runs.

The third (Ruth) and fourth (Gehrig) hitters in the lineup of course wore numbers 3 and 4 on their uniforms. Ruth and Gehrig comprised the most lethal one-two batting combination in the history of baseball. Gehrig won the MVP in 1927 with a slash line of .373/.474/.765 with an OPS of 1.240. Ruth had his record-setting season of 60 home runs. The Babe had 164 RBIs, and scored 158 runs. Ruth did not receive one single vote in the MVP voting. A rule was in place that prevented a previous winner from being eligible. Ruth had won the award in 1923.

Once an opposing pitcher navigated his way through the first four hitters, there was Meusel hitting fifth, followed by the Hall of Famer Lazzeri in the six-hole. Meusel batted .337 that year, with 103 RBIs. Lazzeri drove in 102 runs.

Collins was a 30-year-old veteran catcher who caught 89 games during the season, while 22-game winner, right-hander Waite Hoyt, led the pitching staff. Left-hander Herb Pennock won 19 games and righty Urban Shocker, lefty Dutch Ruether, and right-hander George Pipgras combined for 41 more wins.

Waite Hoyt led the Yankees' 1927 pitching staff with 22 wins.
(George Grantham Bain Collection, Library of Congress)

The most fascinating member of the pitching staff was
side-arming right-hander Wilcy Moore. The 30-year-old was a
rookie in 1927. As a relief pitcher and occasional starter, Moore
appeared in 50 games and pitched 213 innings. He finished
with a 19–7 record, led the American League with 2.28 ERA,
and had 13 saves.

The 1927 Yankees finished with a 110–54 record, setting
a franchise mark with a .714 winning percentage. As a team,
the Yankees hit .307 and led the major leagues with 975 runs
scored. The Detroit Tigers were second with 845 runs scored.
The Yankees led the American League wire to wire, as they won

their first six games of the season. There was no All-Star Game or break in 1927, so the midway point for the Yankees was on July 8th. The team's record at that point was 55–27 (154-game season). They led the American League by 11½ games over the Washington Senators. The Yankees blew the pennant race wide open in mid-August when they won 13 of 17 to extend their lead from 11 to 18 games.

On September 13th, the Yankees swept a doubleheader from the Cleveland Indians at Yankee Stadium to clinch the American League pennant. Ruth homered in both ends of the twin bill for his 52nd of the season. In the opener, Ruth's two-run blast tied the game in the seventh and the Yankees went on to win, 5–3. In Game 2, Ruth went deep in the fourth off Indians left-hander Joe Schaute to tie the game at 2. The Yankees went on to score four en route to another 5–3 win.

On September 30th, the Yankees and Washington Senators were tied at 2 in the bottom of the eighth. After Koenig tripled, Ruth hit a 2–2 pitch that was low and inside and slammed it into the right field stands at Yankee Stadium for his record-setting 60th home run. (Note: In 1927 with a slash line the game, Hall of Fame and Senators pitcher Walter Johnson made his last appearance in a major league game as a pinch-hitter in the ninth inning.)

The Yankees swept the 1927 World Series, outscoring the Pittsburgh Pirates, 23–10, over the four games. In Game 4 the Yankees had the bases loaded and no one out in the bottom of the ninth of a tie game. Gehrig and Meusel struck out, but the game ended when Pirates pitcher Johnny Miljus threw a wild pitch to plate the winning run.

17. On June 20, 1963, the Yankees played an unusual day-night doubleheader.

The Yankees hosted the Washington Senators in the afternoon at Yankee Stadium, and then hosted the New York Mets in the initial "Mayor's Trophy Game" that night. The intracity exhibition was originally scheduled for June 3rd, but it had been rained out and re-scheduled for 17 days later. In the afternoon, the Yankees were trailing the Nats, 4–3, going to the bottom of the ninth. Pinch-hitter Hector Lopez led off the inning with a single. After a sacrifice bunt Tony Kubek singled putting runners on first and third. Bobby Richardson, who was still mourning the death of his father a few days earlier, lined a double into the right-center field gap to score the tying and winning runs in a 5–4 victory. A crowd of 18,915 was in attendance for the afternoon game.

An announced crowd of 50,742, made up mostly of Met fans, was on hand for the night portion of the unique twin bill. It was the first appearance for manager Casey Stengel at Yankee Stadium since he had been fired after the 1960 season. Thirty minutes before the game began, Stengel got a huge ovation when he emerged from the dugout for the first time. Mets fans brought banners, placards, and musical instruments to the game. They were boisterous and they were loud. In the seventh inning, an unidentified minor tossed a smoke bomb between home plate and the pitcher's mound and was arrested. The Mets dressed at the Polo Grounds. On the short bus ride from Manhattan, across the Harlem River, to The Bronx, Stengel encouraged his team to give it their all to get the win.

Stengel was quoted as saying, "This is one you want to win all year. This is the one. If you can win it."

The Mets took a 1–0 lead in the top of the first. Jimmy Piersall led off the game with a double, and eventually came around to score on a wild pitch by Yankees starter Stan

Williams. The Yankees answered with a run in their half of the first on Elston Howard's RBI single. The Mets scored five times in the third inning to blow the game open. An error by Yankees second baseman Pedro Gonzalez with the bases loaded allowed the go-ahead run to score. Tim Harkness singled in two more runs, and the Mets capped off the inning with an RBI double from Al Moran.

There was an incident earlier in the inning. Piersall swung and his bat went flying into the box seats along the third base line. The flying bat hit New York deputy police commissioner William L. Rowe and cracked his ribs. The Yankees were booed throughout the contest. Roger Maris got lustily booed when he flied out as a pinch-hitter in the seventh inning. The Mets went on to win the game, 6–2, but rowdy fans were causing problems even after it was over.

Police were trying to clear the field—in the 1960s, fans were allowed to leave the Stadium through the gates underneath the center field bleachers—as fans were yelling, "It's ours now, we beat 'em." Some of the ushers had to run over to the center field flagpole to prevent some thievish fans from stealing the Yankees world championship banner.

Shea Stadium hosted its first Mayor's Trophy Game in 1964. Over 55,000 fans saw the Yankees get even with a 6–4 win. Roger Maris and Tom Tresh homered in that game along with Joe Pepitone, who hit a ball that caromed off Shea Stadium's right-center field scoreboard.

The 1969 game was scheduled for July 7th (two days before Tom Seaver nearly pitched a perfect game against the Chicago Cubs), but it was rained out and re-scheduled for September 29th at Shea Stadium. By that time, the Mets had already won the National League's Eastern Division title, so they used their starting lineup to prepare for the upcoming playoffs. The Mets beat the Yankees, 7–6, in an exciting game that ended with the tying and go-ahead runs left on base in the ninth when Bobby Murcer bounced out to first. During the game, Yankees relief pitcher Hamilton unleashed his "folly floater" pitch, but Mets center fielder Tommie Agee handled it for a hard-hit single.

18. Babe Ruth was the first of eight Yankees in franchise history to hit a walkoff, grand slam home run.

"The Bambino" was overweight when he showed up for spring training in 1925. In April, he underwent surgery to remove an intestinal abscess.

Ruth did not make his season debut until June 1st. By that time, the Yankees were mired in seventh place, 13½ games out of first place. In late September, the Yankees hosted the Chicago White Sox at Yankee Stadium. Chicago scored three runs in the top of the 10th to grab a 5–2 lead. In the bottom of the 10th, Ruth became the first American Leaguer to hit a walkoff, grand slam home run when he connected off White Sox pitcher Sarge Connally.

Ruth's memorable home run was one of two in franchise history to occur with the team being three runs down. The other time it happened was on May 17, 2002. The Yankees trailed the Minnesota Twins, 9–8, in the bottom of the ninth. Bernie Williams sent the game into extra innings with a two-out home run off Twins relief pitcher Eddie Guardado. It remained tied until the 14th inning, when the Twins plated three runs for a 12–9 lead. In the Yankees' half of the 14th, Jason Giambi, who was 3-for-7 in the game, didn't waste any time as he unloaded on the first pitch from Twins pitcher Mike Trombley with the bases loaded and drove it into the right-center field bleachers for a walkoff grand slam home run (see answer number 11).

In the second game of the 1933 season, Yankees pitcher Red Ruffing hit a walkoff, grand slam home run to beat the Boston Red Sox, 6–2. The Red Sox were victimized again in 1942, when Charlie "King Kong" Keller became the third Yankee to achieve the game-winning achievement. His left-handed swing was expected to be able to take advantage of the short right field porch at Yankee Stadium; however he had a great eye at the plate and could hit to all fields. Keller got the nickname "King Kong" because he was a physically big man with an impressive physique.

In the first game of a 1969 doubleheader against the Washington Senators, Yankees first baseman Joe Pepitone ended it with a walkoff slam in a 7–3 win.

Outfielder Ruppert Jones played only one season with the Yankees, but he is one of the eight to hit a game-ending grand slam home run. In August of 1980, Jones ended the game with a walkoff grand slam home run off Chicago relief pitcher Ed Farmer. Jones, who was acquired from Seattle during the off-season and played only one year in New York, was traded to the San Diego Padres in March of 1981.

Third baseman Mike Pagliarulo had his moment in May of 1987. The Yankees trailed the Minnesota Twins, 7–5, in the bottom of the ninth. Rickey Henderson tied the game with a two-run homer off Twins reliever Jeff Reardon. "Pags" came up with two out and the bases loaded, and lined a ball into the lower right field stands for the game winner.

Alex Rodriguez is the most recent Yankee to have hit a bases clearing walkoff home run. A-Rod joined the list on April 7, 2007, when the Yankees beat the Baltimore Orioles, 8–4.

The Yankees had trailed, 7–6, entering the ninth. With two out and no one on, Robinson Cano singled. Derek Jeter walked, and Bobby Abreu was hit by a pitch to load the bases. Rodriguez hit a 1–2 pitch from Orioles relief pitcher Chris Ray and drove it over the center field wall for the game-winning blast. The home run was a portent of things to come for Rodriguez. A-Rod went on to bat .314 with 54 home runs and 156 RBIs to earn the 2007 American League Most Valuable Player Award.

19. The famous "pine tar game" between the Yankees and Kansas City Royals was played at Yankee Stadium on July 24, 1983, but it did not end until August 18th.

In the top of the ninth, the Yankees led the Royals, 4–3. Kansas City had a man on and two out when Hall of Famer George Brett apparently hit a two-run homer against Yankees closer "Goose" Gossage to give the Royals a 5–4 lead. Yankees manager Billy Martin protested the home run, claiming Brett had used an illegal bat. Martin felt that the pine tar on the bat exceeded the rule that the substance cannot be more than 18" from the handle. Home plate umpire Tim McClelland used home plate (the plate measures 17" across) as a measuring stick, found that the amount of pine tar exceeded the amount allowed by rule and called Brett out. The ruling caused a furor as Brett came storming out of the Royals dugout to animatedly argue the call. The Royals protested the game; four days later American League president Lee MacPhail overruled the umpires and reinstated the home run. In his ruling, the AL president cited the fact that calling Brett out was not in the "spirit of the rule," and that the game would be resumed from that point on August

18th. MacPhail also retroactively ejected Brett for his actions against the umpires. He also ejected Royals manager Dick Howser and pitcher Gaylord Perry, both of whom tried to keep the bat from getting to league officials.

The impending resumption of the game created a distraction. The media swamped the Yankees every day with questions about it, which began to take its toll on the field. There was some doubt the resumption of the game would even take place. A State Supreme Court judge issued a preliminary injunction against resuming the game, but the American League appealed the ruling and the Supreme Court's Appellate Division overturned it.

George Brett and the Yankees were involved in what is arguably the most bizarre play in baseball history, in the "Pine Tar Game." (Courtesy of Missouri State Archives via Wikimedia Commons)

The Royals flew to New York from Kansas City on the day of the resumption, but did not know for certain that they would be playing the game until they got to Yankee Stadium. When the game resumed, the Yankees had made some drastic changes in their defensive lineup. Pitcher Ron Guidry fulfilled a personal fantasy by being posted in center field. Jerry Mumphrey, the starting center fielder when the game was originally played, had been traded to the Houston Astros. Don Mattingly started at first base, but moved to second base for the first time in his major league career. Dave Winfield started in center field and shifted to left field, while the starting left fielder, Steve Kemp, moved to right. Third baseman Graig Nettles and shortstop Roy Smalley were the only two players who started at their positions and remained there when the game resumed 25 days later. Butch Wynegar replaced Rick Cerone as the catcher, and Ken Griffey took over at first base. George Frazier replaced Gossage as the Yankee pitcher in the ninth.

A different umpiring crew was in place for the resumption; they anticipated Martin's ability to try and manipulate the rule book to his advantage. Before another pitch was thrown, Martin had Frazier step off the rubber and throw to first, claiming Brett did not touch the bag. Frazier repeated the effort at second, but both times umpire Dave Phillips signaled safe. When Martin came out to protest, Phillips pulled out an affidavit that was signed by the original four-man umpiring crew stating Brett had touched every base.

A sparse crowd that was reported to be just over 1,200 people saw Frazier strike out Kansas City's Hal McRae for the final out of the ninth. Royals closer Dan Quisenberry was brought in to pitch the bottom of the ninth. When the game was played in July, Quisenberry had not been available because he had pitched five innings the day before.

Having already been ejected back in July, Brett, Howser and Perry were not with the team at Yankee Stadium. Mattingly flied out to center and Smalley struck out. Quisenberry closed the game by getting pinch-hitter Oscar Gamble on a groundball to second.

Having started just after 6 p.m. Eastern Time, the entire event lasted just under 10 minutes.

After part I of the "pine tar game" was played in July, the Yankees had been tied for first place. Following the completion of the game in August, they were in fifth place, 3½ games out.

In December, the rule was amended. If a batter used an illegal bat and got a hit with it, he would not be called out but the bat would be thrown out.

20. Yogi Berra, Bill Dickey, Lou Gehrig, Joe Gordon, Derek Jeter, Babe Ruth, and Gene Woodling are the seven Yankees who have hit .400 or better in multiple World Series.

Five of the seven are already Hall of Famers. (Jeter retired after the 2014 season and will be eligible for the first time on the 2020 ballot.)

Berra, who is considered one of the best catchers of all time, played in 14 World Series and won 10 times. In the 1953 and 1955 World Series, the Yankee catcher hit .429 and .417 respectively. During those two Series, Berra played 13 games and was hitless in only one.

In his very first World Series in 1932, Hall of Famer Bill Dickey hit .438 with seven hits in 16 at-bats. Dickey won seven of the eight World Series that he played in. He batted

.400 (6-for-15) for a second time in 1938, as the Yankees swept the Chicago Cubs in four games. The Louisiana native was an 11-time All-Star during his 17-year Yankee career. Dickey was an integral part of the Yankees team that won four straight World Series championships, from 1936 to 1939. During that four-year run, he averaged .326 and drove in 100 runs in each of the four seasons. Dickey missed the 1943 and 1944 seasons, serving in the military during World War II. He returned for one more season in 1946 and was named the interim manager when Joe McCarthy abruptly resigned in May, but he stepped down with 14 games left in the season. Like Berra, Dickey wore number 8 during his Yankee career, and that single digit is retired in recognition of both players.

Lou Gehrig won six World Series in seven tries with the Yankees. The Hall of Famer is not only one of seven Yankees to hit over .400 in multiple World Series appearances, he's the only Yankee to hit over .500 in multiple appearances. When the Yankees swept the St. Louis Cardinals in four games in the 1928 Series, Gehrig's numbers were off the charts. In four games, Gehrig batted .545 (6-for-11) with four home runs, five runs scored, six runs batted in and nine walks. The Yankees did not get back to the Series until 1932, when Gehrig picked up where he left off. The Yankees first baseman hit .529 with three home runs and eight driven in. As consistent as he was in the regular season, Gehrig was just as consistent in World Series play. The left-handed slugger was a career .361 hitter in the World Series, with an OPS of 1.214.

Former Yankees second baseman Joe Gordon batted .400 in his first World Series, in 1938. Then, in 1941, Gordon hit .500 in the Yankees' five-game victory against the Brooklyn Dodgers.

Derek Jeter was a .321 career hitter in World Series play. The Yankees shortstop hit .409 in the 2000 World Series against the New York Mets and was named the Most Valuable Player. In 2009, Jeter batted .407, setting a personal best with 11 hits in the Series.

Babe Ruth was the first on this list as he hit over .400 in both the 1927 and 1928 World Series. He hit .400 in 1927, but in 1928 he batted an astounding .625, with 10 hits in 16 at-bats.

Outfielder Gene Woodling is the only one on this list who will never be in the Hall of Fame. Woodling played six seasons with the Yankees, but his timing couldn't have been any better. He was a member of the team that won a record five consecutive World Series championships from 1949 to 1953. Woodling hit .400 or better in his first two World Series appearances with the Yankees. In 1949, he batted .400 but played in only three of the five games. The next season, he played in all four games and hit .429 as the Yankees swept the Philadelphia Phillies.

4

HALL OF FAME LEVEL

(Answers appear on page 151.)

You've come a long way from your "rookie" days. Do you have anything left in the tank to get through the most difficult Hall of Fame Level questions?

Close it out. Prove you're worthy of induction into the Yankees fan's Hall of Fame.

1. The Yankees have hit eight home runs in a game twice in franchise history. The first time was in 1939, when six Yankees contributed to the total. Joe DiMaggio and Babe Dahlgren each hit two in that game. The second time was in 2007, when only one Yankee hit two home runs in the game. Name him.

2. On May 24, 1936, Tony Lazzeri became the first American League player to have 11 RBIs in one game, a record that stands to this day. That same game he also became the first player to accomplish another feat. Name that other accomplishment.

3. Match the uniform number on the right with the player who wore it in his first game as a Yankee:
   Don Mattingly   #6
   Mickey Mantle   #38
   Robinson Cano   #18
   Whitey Ford   #14
   Yogi Berra   #46

4. Name the players who made up the "core four" who won five World Series championships in a five-year span.

5. Jim Leyritz tied Game 4 of the 1996 World Series with his memorable three-run home run in the top of the eighth, but who drove in the go-ahead run in the top of the 10th?

6. How many hits did Joe DiMaggio have during his record 56-game hitting streak? Bonus: How many home runs did DiMaggio hit during his record streak?

7. On June 17, 1978, Ron Guidry set a Yankees record when he struck out 18 in a complete game 4–0 win over

the California Angels. How many pitches did he throw in that game?

8. When Don Larsen pitched his perfect game against the Broooklyn Dodgers in Game 5 of the 1956 World Series, how many times did he go to a three-ball count among the 27 batters he faced?

9. The Yankees have had 19 walkoff postseason wins, and 18 players have accounted for these hits. Name the only player to have done it twice with home runs. Double Bonus: How many of the 19 walkoff postseason wins were decided by home runs? How many Yankees pitchers have hit home runs in postseason play?

10. On July 1, 2004, the Yankees played the Boston Red Sox in one of the most exciting regular season games in franchise history. The game is known for Derek Jeter diving into the stands to make a play and coming out with his face all bloodied. The Yankees scored twice in the bottom of the 13th inning to beat Boston, 5–4. Who had the walkoff hit to win the game? Bonus: Who tied the game for the Yankees with a two-out RBI double?

HALL OF FAME LEVEL ANSWERS

1. On July 31, 2007, the Yankees tied a franchise record by hitting eight home runs in one game.

Hideki Matsui was the only Yankee to homer twice in that game. The other Yankees who hit home runs were Bobby Abreu, Melky Cabrera, Robinson Cano, Johnny Damon, Shelley Duncan, and Jorge Posada.

In 2007 the Yankees hosted the Chicago White Sox at Yankee Stadium. In the bottom of the first, Abreu started the barrage with a three-run home run off former Yankees pitcher Jose Contreras. Matsui added a solo shot for his first of the game, and the Yankees led 4–0 after one inning. In the third, Cano hit a three-run home run and Cabrera added a two-run blow. Matsui's second home run came in the sixth off White Sox pitcher Gavin Floyd. The Yankees completed their record-tying output in the seventh, as Damon and Duncan hit solo homers.

Matsui had signed with the Yankees in December of 2002 and joined the team for the 2003 season. The Japanese star, who was nicknamed "Godzilla" for the famous movie monster, hit 332 home runs during his 10-year career in Japan. The Yankees knew that the left-handed power hitter not only would benefit from the short right field porch at Yankee Stadium, he would appeal to the Japanese baseball fans who lived in New York. Matsui's first game in front of the home fans turned out to be a memorable one. It was a cold, damp April day for the 2003 home opener against Minnesota. Temperatures were in the 30s, but the fans were excited to see the team and its new addition from Japan.

Matsui was immediately treated like royalty, beginning with the traditional "roll call" from the "Bleacher Creatures" at Yankee Stadium.

A chant of "MAT-SUI" went on for approximately two minutes. The Japanese star did not realize what was going on at the time, so he did not immediately acknowledge the fans' gesture.

In the bottom of the fifth, the Yankees had runners on second and third with one out. Bernie Williams was intentionally walked to pitch to Matsui, and the stadium crowd got very loud.

With the count full, the 29-year-old drove a changeup into the right-center field bleachers for his first American major league home run. After Matsui descended into the dugout, the fans were still standing and cheering, hoping to get a curtain call from their latest hero. Matsui obliged, appeared from the dugout, and lifted his helmet in tribute. In the 2003 World Series loss to Florida, Matsui became the first Japanese player to hit a home run in a World Series game when he went deep in Game 2.

In 2009, Yankee Stadium II opened and the team got back to the World Series for the first time in six years. In Game 2 against the Philadelphia Phillies, Matsui homered off Pedro Martinez—who was with the Phillies in his final season—to help the Yankees even the Series with a 3–1 win. During the 2009 season, Matsui had been primarily the Yankees' designated hitter, so he didn't start Game 3 in Philadelphia. In the eighth inning, the Yankees led 7–4 when Matsui was sent up to pinch-hit for pitcher Joba Chamberlain. The left-handed hitter delivered a pinch-hit solo home run off Phillies reliever Brett Myers to give the team a little more breathing room in what became a pivotal 8–5 victory.

The Yankees led the Series three games to two when they took the field at Yankee Stadium for Game 6. Matsui, who became a free agent at the end of the season, made his final game in pinstripes a memorable one. First, he hit a two-run home run off Martinez in the second to give the Yankees a 2–0 lead. Then, with the bases loaded in the third, Matsui singled to drive in two more to make it a 4–1 Yankees lead. Matsui came up one more time with the bases loaded in the fifth, and doubled off Phillies lefty J.A. Happ to drive in two more runs, giving him six RBIs for the game.

He would have one final at-bat in the seventh. With a man on first, Matsui struck out but received a thunderous standing ovation in appreciation for not only what he had done in Game 6, but for what he had done throughout his career as a Yankee.

Matsui received the World Series Most Valuable Player Award. He became the first Japanese-born player, and the first full-time designated hitter, to be so honored.

Cano, Damon, and Posada, along with Matsui, were all key components of the 2009 world championship team. Abreu and Duncan played parts of three seasons with the Yankees. Cabrera played parts of five seasons in New York, and was also a member of the 2009 championship team.

2. Hall of Fame second baseman Tony Lazzeri is known for producing one of the greatest single game performances in baseball history.

On May 24, 1936, Lazzeri, who was batting eighth, hit three home runs and drove in a record setting 11 runs in leading the Yankees to a 25–2 rout against the Philadelphia Athletics at Shibe Park.

Lazzeri also became the first player in baseball history to hit two grand slams in the same game. In the top of the second, the 32-year-old got things going with a grand slam off A's pitcher George Turbeville. In the fifth inning, the Yankees continued their run-scoring barrage as Lazzeri set a major league record by hitting a second grand slam to give him eight runs batted in. In the seventh, Lazzeri blasted his third home run and capped off his record-setting day in the eighth with his fourth hit, a two-run triple that gave him 11 RBIs, a mark that still stands as an American League record.

The young infielder had caught the eye of Yankees scout Bill Essick with the astounding numbers that he produced with Salt Lake City in 1925. Lazzeri played in 197 games and batted .355 with 60 home runs and 222 runs batted in, a professional baseball record.

Lazzeri was epileptic and some felt that's why the Chicago Cubs, who had a working agreement with that minor league team, passed on signing him. While he struggled with epilepsy, he never experienced a seizure on the field.

The Yankees acquired Lazzeri after the 1925 season for two players to be named later, and $50,000. At Salt Lake City, Lazzeri was the regular shortstop, but Yankees manager Miller Huggins thought the 22-year-old would be better suited to play second. In his first big league season in 1926, Lazzeri played in all 155 games and put up some impressive numbers. The San Francisco–born Lazzeri had 60 extra-base hits and 117 runs batted in, helping the Yankees win the American League pennant. But it didn't go so well for Lazzeri against the St. Louis Cardinals in the World Series. The Yankees lost in seven games, with Lazzeri batting only .192.

In 1927, Lazzeri found himself on a team that is considered by many to be the greatest of all time. That Yankees team had a lineup that was nicknamed "Murderers' Row" for the firepower that it showcased.

Lazzeri hit sixth behind Babe Ruth, Lou Gehrig, and Bob Meusel; he produced a slash line of .309/.383/.482.

The Yankees second baseman scored 92 runs and drove in 102, yet he finished 11th in the voting for the American League's Most Valuable Player Award.

In the 1927 World Series, Lazzeri hit a modest .267 in the team's four-game sweep of the Pittsburgh Pirates. Lazzeri had his best season in 1929, when he finished fourth in the league in batting with a .354 average.

Being of Italian heritage made Lazzeri very popular among the Italian-Americans who lived in New York. According to Lazzeri's bio, his nickname of "Poosh-'Em up Tony" was created when he played at Salt Lake City. A fan of Italian descent who spoke broken English was rooting for him to get a hit and shouted "Poosh-'Em up Tony."

In the 1932 World Series, Lazzeri hit two home runs in Game 4 to help the Yankees complete a four-game sweep of the Chicago Cubs.

The Yankees would not return to the Series until 1936. In Game 2 against the New York Giants at the Polo Grounds, Lazzeri became the first Yankee to hit a World Series grand slam when he cleared the bases in the third inning. President Franklin D. Roosevelt was at the game when Lazzeri paved the way to an 18–4 rout. Lazzeri played 12 seasons with the Yankees.

After the 1937 season, the talented second baseman was given his unconditional release. He signed with the Chicago Cubs in 1938 and was on the other side of a four-game sweep as he lost to his former team. Lazzeri finished his playing career in 1939 after splitting the season with the Brooklyn Dodgers and the New York Giants. He was inducted into the Baseball Hall of Fame by the Veterans Committee in 1991.

3. Don Mattingly's number 23 is one of 20 uniform numbers (for 21 players) that are retired and on display in Yankee Stadium's Monument Park, but he wore number 46 when he debuted in the major leagues as a defensive replacement in the outfield on September 8, 1982.

The 21-year-old began the 1983 season with the big club, but was sent to its AAA affiliate at Columbus in mid-April.

After Bobby Murcer announced his retirement in June of 1983, Mattingly was brought back up from the minors to take his spot on the roster. In 1984, the Yankees first baseman and teammate Dave Winfield were locked in an emotional and bittersweet pursuit of the American League batting title. In the final game Mattingly had four hits to improve to .343, while Winfield had only one hit and dropped to .340. In addition to the batting title, Mattingly led the league with 207 hits and 44 doubles.

In a baseball version of "Can you top this?," Mattingly was even better in 1985.

The Indiana native won the American League's Most Valuable Player Award, and his numbers were off the charts, as he batted .324 with 35 home runs and 145 runs batted in.

Mattingly continued his consistent offensive production in 1986. The Yankees first baseman batted .352 with 31 home runs, 113 RBIs, and a league-leading 238 hits.

From 1984 to 1986 many people around baseball were calling Mattingly the best player in the game. The 25-year-old slammed 89 home runs over three seasons, but his power numbers peaked in 1987 when he tied one home run mark and set another.

On July 18th, in Arlington, Texas, Mattingly tied the all-time mark by hitting a home run in his eighth straight game. On September 28th, the Yankees hosted the Boston Red Sox. In the bottom of the third, Mattingly set a major league record (that has since been tied by Cleveland Indians designated hitter Travis Hafner, in 2006) by hitting his sixth grand slam home run of the season.

The irony of Mattingly's record-setting season in 1987 is that he had not hit a grand slam home run before that season, nor did he hit one after that.

Unfortunately, Mattingly's decline began in 1990. A disc problem in his back was beginning to impede his ability to hit a baseball. 1995 would be his final season, but he went out with a bang. The Yankees won the first American League Wild Card berth. After all his years of missing out on the postseason, Mattingly was finally going to the playoffs. In Game 2 against Seattle in the American League Divisional Series, Mattingly hit his only postseason home run. The Yankees trailed the Mariners, 2–1, in the bottom of the sixth when Ruben Sierra led off the inning with a game-tying home run to right field against Seattle starter Andy Benes. The sellout crowd of 57,126 at Yankee Stadium had barely settled down when Mattingly drove a 1–0 pitch into the right-center field bleachers. The stadium literally shook as Mattingly rounded the bases. The Yankees lost the Series in five games, but Mattingly acquitted himself very well in his only postseason appearance.

In the five games, Mattingly hit .417 (10 for 24) with a home run and six runs batted in.

The six-time All-Star and nine-time Gold Glove winner did not officially announce his retirement until January of 1997. Mattingly's number 23 was retired by the Yankees on August 31, 1997.

Nineteen-year-old Mickey Mantle wore number 6 when he made his major league debut on April 17, 1951. Mantle became famous wearing number 7, but reportedly the clubhouse manager, Pete Sheehy, thought the young switch-hitter would be the next in line after Babe Ruth's number 3, Lou Gehrig's number 4 and Joe DiMaggio's number 5, so he originally issued uniform number 6. The Oklahoma native was famous for hitting majestic home runs that would transfix the sports world. On April 17, 1953, the Yankees were playing the Washington Senators at Griffith Stadium, a ballpark that was considered a pitcher friendly park. With Yogi Berra on first and two out in the top of the fifth, Mantle faced Senators left-center Chuck Stobbs. Batting right-handed, Mantle launched a tremendous blast toward left-center field. The ball sailed way over the 391-foot sign in left-center field and went past a huge sign that featured a mascot of a beer company. It ended up clipping the mascot's mustache and continued to soar past the rooftops of houses, finally landing across neighboring Fifth Street. Yankees public relations director Red Patterson found a 10-year-old with the ball and the youngster showed him where the ball landed. Contrary to popular belief, Patterson did not use a tape measure. Instead, he figured the distance by "using the dimensions of the park, its walls and the distance he paced off." Patterson calculated the ball traveled a distance of 565 feet.

On two occasions, Mantle nearly hit a ball completely out of Yankee Stadium. In Game 1 of a doubleheader vs. the Senators, on May 30, 1956, right-hander Pedro Ramos was on the mound for Washington. In the bottom of the fifth, with two on and two out, Mantle smacked a high drive that headed toward the right field upper deck. The ball appeared to have a chance to leave the Stadium, but it slammed against the right field façade, a reported 18" from clearing the roof.

The second time occurred nearly seven years from that day. On May 22, 1963, the Yankees hosted the Kansas City Athletics. The game was tied at 7 in the bottom of the 11th inning, and Mantle was the leadoff batter facing A's right-hander Bill Fischer. Mantle then hit a ball that he would later call "the hardest ball I ever hit." The switch-hitter, batting left-handed, unloaded a high, majestic drive that seemed destined to become the first to be completely hit out of Yankee Stadium. The ball hit the facade just mere inches from the top and bounded back onto the infield.

Mantle hit the façade three times in his career. There were unconfirmed reports that he actually did manage to hit the ball out of the stadium a number of times during batting practice sessions.

Mantle announced his retirement in March of 1969. On June 8, 1969, more than 61,000 fans were on hand to honor their beloved star on Mickey Mantle Day as the Yankees retired his number 7. At that time, there were only three other retired numbers: Babe Ruth's number 3, Lou Gehrig's number 4, and Joe DiMaggio's number 5.

Robinson Cano wore number 14 when he debuted for the Yankees on May 3, 2005. Cano wore that number for fewer than 10 games, then switched to number 22. Following the 2006 season, Cano wore number 24 for the remainder of his Yankee career. Cano, who was named after Hall of Famer Jackie Robinson, began the 2005 season at the Yankees' AAA affiliate at Columbus; he was hitting .330 when he got called up. Over the next eight seasons, Cano would develop into one of the best second basemen in baseball. During the 2009 season, the Dominican Republic native played all but one game in the entire season as he helped the Yankees win their 27th World Series championship. Cano batted .309 over his nine-year stint with the Yankees. During his time in The Bronx, he was a five-time All-Star, five-time Silver Slugger Award winner, and received two Gold Gloves.

A short time after Whitey Ford was inducted into the Baseball Hall of Fame in 1974, the Yankees retired his number 16. When the left-hander from Queens, New York, made his major league debut in July of 1950, he wore number 18. The crafty southpaw also wore number 19 during his first season. Ford missed two years while serving in the Korean War; when he came back in time for the 1953 season, he was issued his familiar number 16.

Yogi Berra wore number 38 in his first year of 1946. The Hall of Fame catcher was a September call-up and only played seven games. Berra took uniform number 35 in his second year, but he started to wear the famous number 8 in his third season of 1948. Berra is considered one of the greatest all-around catchers in the history of baseball. He won three American League Most Valuable Player Awards and was a 15-time All-Star. The St. Louis native played in a record 14 World Series while winning a record 10 times. In Game 5 of the 1956 World Series against the Brooklyn Dodgers, Berra caught Don Larsen's perfect game. In Game 7, the Yankees catcher hit a pair of two-run homers in the first and third innings to set the tone. The Yankees went on to win the game, 9–0, and avenge their World Series loss to Brooklyn the year before. Berra retired as a player after the 1963 season and managed the team in 1964. The Hall of Famer returned to the Yankees as a coach in 1976, had a second managerial stint in 1984 that lasted sixteen games in 1985.

4. Pitchers Andy Pettitte and Mariano Rivera, along with catcher Jorge Posada and shortstop Derek Jeter, were nick-named the "core four" because they were homegrown Yankees who played together for a long time.

All four made their major league debuts in 1995. Three of them (Pettitte, Rivera and Jeter) debuted within a month of each other. Pettitte made his first major league start on May 27th in Oakland, and then joined the rotation for the remain-der of the season. The 6'5" left-hander from Deer Park, Texas, won 12 games in his first big league season, finishing third in the voting for the Rookie of the Year award. The Texas native got his first taste of postseason play when he started and pitched a respectable seven innings in Game 2 of the American League Divisional Series against Seattle.

Pettitte was known for picking off runners at first base with his superior ability to stymie the opponents' running game. He also developed a reputation as a clutch postseason pitcher.

In Game 5 of the 1996 World Series, Pettitte pitched one of the best clutch games in franchise history. The left-hander tossed shutout ball into the ninth inning to lead the Yankees to a 1–0 win over Hall of Famer John Smoltz and the Atlanta Braves.

From 1998 through the 2001 American League Championship Series (when he won the Most Valuable Player Award), Pettitte won 11 straight postseason starts. Following the 2003 season Pettitte left the Yankees as a free agent, but he returned in 2007. During his second tenure, Pettitte was part of another championship rotation in 2009. He retired after the 2010 season, but came back after missing one season to pitch in 2012 and 2013. During his fifteen seasons with the Yankees, Pettitte won 219 games.

Mariano Rivera began his career as a starter. He went into the record books 652 saves later as the greatest closer in the history of baseball. In May of 1995, the native of Panama had a rough debut as he gave up five runs in 3⅓ innings pitched against the California Angels. Rivera's talent came to the forefront on July 4th. The 25-year-old pitched eight innings and struck out 11 in a win over the Chicago White Sox. After making what would turn out to be the final start of his career in early September, the lanky right-hander began to carve out his career as a reliever. Working as the set-up reliever for closer John Wetteland, Rivera burst into stardom in 1996. On May 17th, Rivera recorded the first save of his career at Yankee Stadium with a scoreless inning against the Angels. He pitched two or more innings in 35 games as the Yankees launched the lethal one-two combo to capture the World Series.

Rivera replaced Wetteland (who left as a free agent after the 1996 season) as the team's closer in 1997. Using his famed "cutter" pitch, Rivera went on to dominate the sport. The Yankees won four more championships with the Panamanian as their closer. On September 19, 2011, Rivera set an all-time record when he recorded career save number 602 against the Minnesota Twins at Yankee Stadium. Rivera played 19 seasons with the Yankees and ended his career following the 2013 season. His number 42 had already been retired by Major League Baseball in honor of Jackie Robinson, but he was allowed to continue wearing it and became the last player to wear that number.

Jorge Posada began his professional career as an infielder. While playing in the Yankees minor league system at Oneonta in 1991, the switch-hitter was primarily a second baseman. It was deemed by the Yankees that Posada's future as a second baseman was limited, so the team proposed that the native of Puerto Rico be turned into a catcher. The switch-hitting catcher was called up in September of 1995 and placed on the playoff roster. Posada scored a run as a pinch-runner in Game 2 against Seattle. He played in only eight games in 1996 and was not on the playoff roster. Joe Girardi was the starting catcher, but Posada succeeded Jim Leyritz as the backup with an eye toward eventually securing the everyday job.

Following a breakout 1998 season, when he hit 17 home runs and drove in 63, Posada became the full-time catcher in 1999. The switch-hitter played his entire 17-year career with the Yankees and had two signature moments. In 1998, Posada caught David Wells's perfect game. In Game 7 of the 2003 American League Championship Series vs. Boston, Posada's bloop double off Boston Red Sox starter Pedro Martinez tied the game at 5 in the eighth inning, helping the Yankees to rally from a 5–2 deficit.

In the 1992 amateur draft, the Yankees had the sixth overall selection and used it to tab 17-year-old shortstop Derek Jeter from Kalamazoo, Michigan. Jeter went on to become the franchise's all-time hits leader and the best shortstop in Yankees history. The 14-time All-Star produced some magical moments in a Yankees uniform, beginning with his first game as the starting shortstop in 1996. The Yankees opened the season in Cleveland, where Jeter hit his first major league home run off Indians pitcher Dennis Martinez. He also made a spectacular over-the-shoulder catch of a short pop fly that became a signature play for the young shortstop.

In Game 1 of the 1996 American League Championship Series against Baltimore, Jeter hit a controversial home run. With the Yankees trailing, 4–3, in the bottom of the eighth, Jeter lined a ball toward the right field wall. It appeared that Orioles right fielder Tony Tarasco would have enough room to catch the ball. A fan named Jeffrey Maier reached over with his glove and caught the ball. Right field umpire Rich Garcia ruled it a home run that tied the game at 4. The Yankees won the game and went on to win the World Series in Jeter's first full season. The 21-year-old was also named a unanimous winner of the American League Rookie of the Year Award.

In 2000, Jeter became the first player to be named both the All-Star Game MVP and the World Series MVP in the same season.

On September 11, 2009, Jeter lined a trademark single to right field. It gave him 2,722 career hits, surpassing Lou Gehrig for the most in Yankees history. No Yankee had ever reached the coveted mark of 3,000 hits, but Jeter was two hits shy of that mark when the Yankees hosted the Tampa Bay Rays on September 9, 2011. In the bottom of the first, Jeter singled to left to move within one hit of 3,000. In his next at-bat, in the bottom of the third, Jeter smacked a solo home run off Rays lefty David Price, into the left-center field stands.

Jeter lived up to his reputation of seizing the moment when he became the second player in baseball history to hit a home run for career hit number 3,000. (Wade Boggs was the first in 1999, when he played with Tampa Bay. Alex Rodriguez became the third in 2015.)

In his final season, 2014, Jeter went out with a bang. In his final home game, Jeter hit a walkoff RBI single in the bottom of the ninth to beat the Baltimore Orioles, 6–5. Jeter played his entire 20-year career with the Yankees. He finished with 3,465 hits and a .310 career batting average.

5. Hall of Fame third baseman Wade Boggs walked as a pinch-hitter with the bases loaded in the top of the 10th to drive in the go-ahead run in Game 4 of the 1996 World Series against the Atlanta Braves.

The Yankees had dropped the first two games of the series at home, but won Game 3 in Atlanta. In Game 4 the Braves took an early 6–0 lead, but the Yankees tied the game on Jim Leyritz's three-run home run off Braves closer Mark Wohlers in the eighth. In the top of the 10th, the Yankees had runners at first and second with two out against Atlanta lefty reliever Steve Avery. Braves manager Bobby Cox made a surprising decision to intentionally walk Bernie Williams to load the bases and pitch to left-handed batter Andy Fox. (Williams was 2-for-16 at that point of the Series, but he was a much better hitter from the right side.)

It was an unconventional move but Yankees manager Joe Torre countered with Boggs, who was known for his astute knowledge of the strike zone. The Yankees pinch-hitter would not go out of the zone to swing at a pitch; he took ball one. Avery came back with a strike on the outside corner to even the count at one and one. With the count at one ball and two strikes, the Braves left-hander threw a wicked slider that just missed low and away, as Boggs checked his swing. Boggs worked the count to three balls and two strikes. On the sixth pitch of the at-bat, Avery went up high but the Yankee pinch-hitter laid off the pitch and the Yankees took a 7–6 lead. It turned into one of the most celebrated walks in Yankees history. The Yankees won that game and the next two to capture their first world championship in 18 years.

The Hall of Fame third baseman Boggs had been an integral part of the Yankees/Red Sox rivalry ever since he made his major league debut in 1982. On July 4, 1983, Yankee pitcher Dave Righetti struck out Boggs for the final out of his no-hitter. Boggs and Yankee first baseman Don Mattingly were constantly being measured up against each other because they were both such great hitters. When he won the American League's Most Valuable Player Award in 1985, Don Mattingly finished third in the league in batting, while Boggs won his second batting crown. In 1986, both players were locked in a tight race for the batting championship that went right down to the wire. The Red Sox hosted the Yankees in a season-ending four-game series. Boggs was at .357, and Mattingly was hitting .350 when the series began.

The Red Sox were heading to the playoffs as American League East champs and the games meant nothing to them in the standings, so Boggs sat out the entire four games claiming he was resting his injured hamstring.

Mattingly raised his average to .352, but Boggs's average didn't change, so he won his second consecutive American League batting title and third overall.

Boggs was widely considered to be one of the best hitters of his era, one who could possibly have flirted with a .400 average. For each of seven straight seasons with Boston, Boggs recorded 200 or more hits. In 1992, at the age of 32, Boggs finished with the lowest batting average of his career when he hit .259. Boston management was ready to move on, and Boggs became a free agent. After third baseman Charlie Hayes was taken in the expansion draft by the new National League franchise in Colorado, the Yankees needed to fill that position.

Yankees owner George Steinbrenner overruled general manager Gene Michael and manager Buck Showalter, and signed Boggs to a three-year, $11 million contract. What Michael and Showalter failed to realize at the time was how Boggs would help change the philosophy of the Yankees offense. Boggs's patience and discipline at the plate rubbed off on the rest of the team and helped set the tone for what was to come in later years. During his four-year stay with the Yankees, Boggs was a four-time All Star and won his only two Gold Glove Awards.

Leyritz made his way through the Yankees farm system and debuted in 1990. Primarily a catcher, Leyritz also played some games at third base and first base, but he was known for being a clutch player who hit some big home runs. The home run in Game 4 of the 1996 World Series was Leyritz's signature moment, but a year earlier he had put his stamp on a memorable postseason game at Yankee Stadium. The Yankees were playing the Seattle Mariners in Game 2 of the newly created, best-of-five Divisional Series. The Yankees won Game 1, and Game 2 was tied at 4 in extra innings. In the 12th Seattle took a 5–4 lead. The Yankees tied the game on Ruben Sierra's two-out, RBI double, but the inning ended when Bernie Williams, who would have scored the winning run, was thrown out at the plate. In the bottom of the 15th, Yankees second baseman Pat Kelly walked with one out, bringing up a fatigued Leyritz.

The Yankee catcher had been behind the plate for all 15 innings when he batted against Mariners relief pitcher Tim Belcher. On a 3–1 pitch, Leyritz hit a game-winning home run that landed over the right centerfield wall, sending the Stadium crowd into a frenzy.

The Yankees won the game, 7–5. Unfortunately, they would go on to lose the next three games in Seattle.

After nine years with the Yankees, Leyritz was traded to the Anaheim Angels following the 1996 season.

6. Joe DiMaggio accumulated 91 hits during his record streak of hitting in 56 consecutive games in 1941.

The streak began on May 15th when the Yankees hosted the Chicago White Sox and DiMaggio singled in the bottom of the first. The next day, the Yankees beat the White Sox, 6–5, by scoring two in the bottom of the ninth. DiMaggio had a triple to start the late-inning rally, and his first home run during the streak. It took a little luck to keep the streak going. On June 17th, DiMaggio got his only base hit of the game on a groundball that took a bad hop and bounced off Chicago White Sox shortstop Luke Appling's shoulder. The hit also gave DiMaggio a 30-game hitting streak to set a Yankees franchise record.

In late June, the Yankees played the Washington Senators in a doubleheader at Griffith Stadium. In the opener, DiMaggio extended his streak to 41 straight games with a sixth-inning double. The hit also tied George Sisler's American League record.

"The Yankee Clipper" was shooting for a new American League mark in the second game, but he got thrown for a loop when he discovered someone had apparently stolen his lucky bat. An usher told DiMaggio that an unidentified person had leaned over the railing, lifted the bat, and disappeared into the crowd. In his next to last at-bat, DiMaggio singled to extend his streak to 42 straight games and break Sisler's mark. Word was put out through radio and the newspapers that DiMaggio was hoping for someone to return his bat. It was discovered that the man who stole the bat lived in Newark, New Jersey, and was using it in a public display. According to *DiMaggio, Setting the Record Straight*, by Morris Engelberg and Marv Schneider, "DiMaggio had friends in Newark and they were pleased to be able to do Joe a favor."

Joe DiMaggio during his hitting streak in 1941. (Library of Congress)

DiMaggio was two games shy of tying Wee Willie Keeler's record of hitting in 44 straight games. The Yankees hosted brother Dom DiMaggio and the Boston Red Sox in a doubleheader on July 1st. In the opening contest, DiMaggio singled in the fifth to pull within one game of Keeler's mark. "Joltin' Joe" took care of business in his very first at-bat in Game 2, and it's a good thing he did. DiMaggio singled in the first to tie the record of 44 straight games. The game was called because of rain and darkness after five innings, with the Yankees leading, 9–2.

The next day, DiMaggio set a new record by hitting a two-run home run.

Following the All-Star break, the Yankees were playing the St. Louis Browns at Sportsman's Park. In the top of the first, DiMaggio singled to extend his streak to 49 consecutive games. Once again, weather played a factor and the game was called after five innings, with the Yankees shutting out the hapless Browns, 1–0. In the final two games of the three-game series, DiMaggio was 6 for 10 as the streak reached 51 straight games.

After a doubleheader sweep on July 13th in Chicago, the Yankees were riding a 14-game winning streak. DiMaggio's personal streak now reached 53 in a row. A loss the next day ended the Yanks' winning streak, but DiMaggio still kept his personal streak going with an infield hit. On July 15th, DiMaggio added three more hits and extended the streak to 55 in a row. The following day, before 12,000 people at Cleveland's League Park (the Indians played a number of home games at League Park that season), DiMaggio had three hits to reach 56 consecutive games.

On July 17th, over 67,000 fans jammed Cleveland's Municipal Stadium to see if DiMaggio could keep the streak going, or if they would be witness to history by watching it come to an end.

In the top of the first, DiMaggio lined a ball toward the third base line. Indians third baseman Ken Keltner was playing deep and was able to backhand the ball and throw out DiMaggio at first by a step.

In the fourth the "Yankee Clipper" walked, and then in the seventh Keltner made another nice play to rob DiMaggio again.

He would have one more chance in the eighth, but the streak ended when DiMaggio bounced into an inning-ending doubleplay.

During the streak, DiMaggio raised his batting average from .306 to .375. His total of 91 hits included 56 singles, 16 doubles, 4 triples, and 15 home runs. During the streak the Yankees went 41–15 and had a six-game lead over Cleveland for first place in the American League.

Baseball historians consider Joe DiMaggio one of the greatest players of all time. His first big league game, on May 3, 1936, was a huge event with the large Italian community in New York City. There were many among the 25,000 on hand at Yankee Stadium to see their newest hero. In his first game he was in left field, batting third, in front of first baseman Lou Gehrig. He didn't disappoint. "Joltin' Joe" had three hits, including a triple and a run batted in as the Yankees beat the St. Louis Browns, 14–5. DiMaggio hit a league-leading .381 in 1939 and won his second MVP Award. In the World Series that year, DiMaggio got the key hit in Game 4 to give the Yankees a sweep of the Cincinnati Reds. The Yankees and Reds were tied at 4 in the top of the 10th of Game 4 at Cincinnati's Crosley Field. With runners at first and third and one out,

DiMaggio singled to right to bring home Frank Crosetti with the go-ahead run. Reds right fielder Ival Goodman booted the ball, and Charlie Keller scored from first when the relay throw to home plate was dropped by Reds catcher Ernie Lombardi.

Lombardi, who was 6'3", fell down trying to catch the throw and the ball rolled a few feet away. DiMaggio was an instinctive player; he saw an opening and scored (what is referred to as a "Little League home run") on the second miscue, as the Yankees went on to a 7–4 win.

In 1949, DiMaggio missed the first 65 games of the season because of a bone spur in his heel. He was in constant pain, until it suddenly went away. DiMaggio made his season debut on June 28th and hit four home runs in three games to power a sweep against the Red Sox and open an eight-game lead for the team.

Boston rallied later in the season to lead the Yankees by a game heading into a final, two-game, head-to-head showdown at Yankee Stadium. The first game was played on Joe DiMaggio Day, but the Yankee Clipper was physically and emotionally spent. Despite that, he doubled and scored a run in their 5–4 win that forced a do-or-die finale the next day.

The Yankees led 5–0 in the ninth, but a tired DiMaggio could not make a play on a drive that went for a two-run triple. At that point he removed himself from the game, and the Yankees held on to win the American League pennant.

DiMaggio played 13 seasons with the Yankees and was an All-Star in every one of them. The Hall of Famer retired after the 1951 season.

7. Ron Guidry threw 138 pitches when he struck out 18 to set a franchise record in 1978.

The Yankees southpaw gave up four hits, walked two, and faced 33 batters. Guidry's gem broke the previous Yankees record set by Whitey Ford and Bob Shawkey. In April of 1959, Ford had struck out 15 batters as he pitched 14 innings in blanking the Washington Senators, 1–0. Shawkey struck out 15 in a nine-inning game in 1919.

For a pitcher who stood 5'11" and weighed 161 pounds, Guidry could throw surprisingly hard. Yankees reliever Sparky Lyle taught Guidry how to throw a slider. When the southpaw added that pitch to his repertoire, his career took off.

The Louisiana native had a breakout season in 1977 when he won 16 games, including Game 4 of the 1977 World Series. In 1978, Guidry was off to a 10–0 start when he faced the California Angels on June 17th in a Saturday night game at Yankee Stadium. In the first inning, Guidry struck out the Angels' Rick Miller and Joe Rudi. The Yankees scored a run in the first and Guidry ended the second with his third strikeout of the game. In the third, the Yankees southpaw escaped a two-on, two-out jam when he struck out Rudi (Guidry's third of the inning) for a second time. Guidry struck out the side in the fourth and had nine for the game.

When Guidry got two strikes on a batter, the crowd of 33,162 began a rhythmic clap to spur him on to record another strikeout. (This game is widely credited with being the start of the "two-strike rhythmic clap.")

On the TV broadcast, Yankees announcer Phil Rizzuto began referring to Guidry as "Louisiana Lightning," in honor of his heritage. He was also called "Gator."

In the fifth inning, Guidry struck out two more and then fanned the side in the sixth to give him 14 strikeouts after six innings. He was one away from tying the franchise record. In the seventh, Angels third baseman Ron Jackson flied to right and Merv Rettenmund grounded out to third base. Guidry appeared to be getting weary, but he tied the franchise record when he struck out catcher Brian Downing for a second time.

"Louisiana Lightning" set a new franchise mark by striking out Ike Hampton to lead off the eighth. That gave him 16, and a shot at the major league record of 19 if he could get three strikeouts in the ninth.

Guidry got back-to-back strikeouts to begin the ninth. Don Baylor singled to center field. The crowd cheered because they wanted to see Guidry tie the record. It wasn't meant to be, as Jackson hit a grounder to third, forcing Baylor at second to end the game.

On July 19th, the Yankees trailed the Boston Red Sox by 14 games in the American League East. The Yankees won eight of their next nine games to begin the comeback. Within that span, Guidry won back-to-back complete game shutouts to improve to 15–1, and pulling the Yankees to within 9½ games of Boston. After pitching a "no-decision," Guidry lost his second game of the season in early August, hurling a complete game and giving up just one earned run in a 2–1 defeat.

"Gator" then went on to win seven straight decisions, including the last two of the club's streak against the Red Sox. In both of those games, Guidry went the distance on complete game shutouts. The first was the third game of the so-called "Boston Massacre" at Fenway Park. Six days later, Guidry tossed a two-hitter as the Yankees took a 2½-game lead in the division in mid-September. "Louisiana Lightning" lost his next start, but won his final two outings of the regular season, bringing his record to 24–3.

Yankees manager Bob Lemon wanted his ace left-hander available to start a one-game playoff if needed, so he set his rotation accordingly down the stretch. The Yankees lefty gave up two runs in 6⅓ innings, pitching on three days rest, to help the Yankees win that memorable game. Guidry got his 25th win (for statistical purposes, the game counted as a regular season game) and finished 25–3.

The southpaw set a franchise record with an .893 winning percentage and a 1.74 ERA, a record for Yankee left-handers. In the 1978 World Series against the Los Angeles Dodgers, Guidry pitched a complete game win in Game 3 at Yankee Stadium after the Yankees had lost the first two. "Gator" benefited from the defense of Yankees third baseman Graig Nettles, who made a number of outstanding plays to save the game.

Guidry played his entire 14-year career with the Yankees and won 170 games. He retired after the 1988 season. His number 49 was retired by the Yankees in 2003.

8. In Game 5 of the 1956 World Series, Yankees right-hander Don Larsen pitched the first perfect game in World Series history, blanking the Brooklyn Dodgers, 2–0.

Larsen set down 27 batters on 97 pitches. He went to a three-ball count only once in the entire game. That was in the very first inning when the second batter of the game, Dodgers shortstop Pee Wee Reese, worked a 3–2 count. Reese was caught looking at a called third strike, as was the leadoff batter before him, Dodgers second baseman Jim Gilliam.

Larsen retired Duke Snider on a line drive to right, and had thrown 15 pitches in the first inning. In the second, Jackie Robinson lined a ball off Yankees third baseman Andy Carey, but it caromed over to shortstop Gil McDougald, who threw out the speedy Dodger. After three innings, Larsen and his counterpart, Dodgers pitcher Sal "the Barber" Maglie, had both set down the first nine hitters. Larsen threw 33 pitches over the first three innings. Interestingly, he also threw 33 over the next three innings.

Maglie set down two more Yankees in the bottom of the fourth before Mickey Mantle lined a 2–2 pitch into the lower right field stands for a 1–0 lead. It was the Yankees' switch-hitter's eighth World Series home run.

In the Dodgers' fifth, Larsen got Robinson on a deep fly ball to left field. The 6'4" right hander was beginning to get the ball up in the strike zone, and the next batter nearly spoiled the day. Gil Hodges hit a line drive headed toward the left-center field gap that appeared to be the first Brooklyn hit, but Mantle went streaking over and made a terrific backhanded grab to preserve the historic gem. Sandy Amoros followed with a deep fly to right that went foul; he eventually hit a grounder for the 18th consecutive out.

In the top of the sixth, Maglie made Larsen work for his penultimate strikeout of the game. The Brooklyn pitcher did not have any World Series hits in his career, but he made Larsen throw seven pitches before he struck out.

The Yankees added a second run in their half of the sixth. Carey led off with a single and was sacrificed to second by Larsen with a two-strike bunt. Hank Bauer's single drove in Carey. Larsen was at 66 pitches (was that an omen?) as he entered the seventh inning. The 6'4" right-hander used only eight pitches in the seventh to set down Gilliam, Reese, and Snider for a third time.

After the seventh, none of his Yankees teammates would even talk to Larsen in the dugout (a superstition among base-ball players when their pitcher is working on a no-hit game) but Larsen said to Mantle, "Look at the scoreboard, Mick, wouldn't it be something?" Mantle did not answer and walked away.

After Larsen retired Robinson on a groundball for the first out of the eighth, Hodges lined a bullet to Carey. The third baseman made a shoestring catch for the out but threw to first just to make sure, in case the umpire had signaled safe.

With that out, Larsen set a new World Series record by retiring his 23rd straight batter to start the game. In Game 3 of the 1927 World Series against Pittsburgh, Yankees southpaw Herb Pennock had set down the first 22 Pirate hitters.

A packed house of 64,519 at Yankee Stadium was on the edge of their seats for the ninth inning. Larsen's pitch count was at 84 as he took the mound for the fateful ninth inning. In the ninth, Dodgers outfielder Carl Furillo battled Larsen for six pitches and flied out to deep right field for the first out. Catcher Roy Campanella grounded to second on an 0–1 pitch to become the 26th consecutive out. Dodgers manager Walter Alston sent up pinch-hitter Dale Mitchell to bat for Maglie. The Dodgers' right-hander had pitched an outstanding game himself, but he was on the short end of history. Mitchell was a left-handed hitter who was not prone to striking out. Larsen threw ball one, then got a called strike to even the count. Mitchell swung through the third pitch and then fouled off the next one. The count was 1–2 when Larsen threw his 97th pitch of the game. Home plate umpire Babe Pinelli, who was retiring after the game, called strike three on Mitchell and the crowd roared to a pitch that had not been heard before in The Bronx.

Berra rushed out to the mound and famously leaped into Larsen's arms as the entire Yankees team mobbed the newest hero.

After the game, Larsen was understandably mobbed in the Yankees clubhouse. Even their opponent was impressed with what had just occurred. According to the Associated Press, Dodgers president Walter O'Malley came into the Yankees room and congratulated Larsen. "You beat us and I'm not happy about that," O'Malley said. "Do me a favor, will you? Sign this ball."

Larsen was a journeyman pitcher who had been traded to the Yankees from the Baltimore Orioles as part of a 17-player deal. He was later traded to the Kansas City Athletics in 1959 as part of a deal that brought back Roger Maris.

Larsen retired after appearing in three games for the Chicago Cubs in 1967.

9. Center fielder Bernie Williams is the only player in Yankees history to have two postseason walkoff home runs.

In Game 1 of the 1996 American League Championship Series, Williams hit a solo home run off Baltimore Orioles pitcher Randy Myers in the bottom of the 11th inning to give the Yankees a 5–4 win. Three years later, in Game 1 of the 1999 ALCS against Boston, Williams homered off Red Sox reliever Rod Beck in the bottom of the 10th inning.

Williams was a key member of four championship teams. The native of Puerto Rico was the starting point for the influx of young talent that would become the core of the championship run. Williams debuted in 1991 and became the everyday center fielder in 1993. In 1998, the switch-hitter batted .342 to become the first player in major league history to win a batting title, Gold Glove and World Series ring in the same season. Following that season, Williams became a free agent. It was becoming increasingly apparent that he was going to leave the

Yankees and sign with the rival Red Sox. Boston made an offer of seven years, topping the Yankees' original offer of five years, $60 million. Anticipating Williams's departure, the Yankees were in negotiations with enigmatic free agent slugger Albert Belle.

At the last minute Williams called Yankees owner George Steinbrenner and told him how much it meant to him to be a Yankee. Steinbrenner reversed field and came up with a seven year, $87.5 million contract to keep Williams in the Bronx for the remainder of his career.

The first Yankees postseason walkoff hit came in Game 1 of the 1939 World Series. The Yankees were tied 1–1 with the Cincinnati Reds. Bill Dickey singled in the bottom of the ninth to score the winning run. The Hall of Fame catcher spent his entire 17-year career with the Yankees.

A home run has ended a postseason game 12 times in franchise history. The first time was in the 1949 World Series against the Brooklyn Dodgers. In Game 1, Tommy Henrich hit a home run to deep right field off Hall of Fame pitcher Don Newcombe to break up a scoreless tie in a thrilling 1–0 win.

Mickey Mantle hit a famous, record-setting walkoff home run in Game 3 of the 1964 World Series against the St. Louis Cardinals. The game was tied at 1 in the bottom of the ninth. Mantle led off the inning against Cardinals knuckleball pitcher Barney Schultz. On the first pitch, the switch-hitting slugger, batting left-handed, hit a majestic home run off Schultz's knuckleball that bounced off the facade of the upper deck. With that game-winning blow, Mantle broke Babe Ruth's World Series record by notching his 16th career home run in the Fall Classic.

Chris Chambliss and Aaron Boone each hit Series-clinching walkoff home runs. Chambliss beat the Kansas City Royals in Game 5 of the 1976 American League Championship Series with a ninth inning walkoff home run. Boone's historic blast came in the bottom of the 11th of Game 7 of the ALCS vs. the Boston Red Sox. In Game 2 of the 1995 American League Divisional Series against Seattle, Jim Leyritz hit a two-run homer in the bottom of the 15th to beat the Mariners, 7–5. Chad Curtis joined the list when he hit a solo home run in the bottom of the 10th to give the Yankees a 6–5 win over the Atlanta Braves in Game 3 of the 1999 World Series.

Seattle was victimized again when Alfonso Soriano hit a two-run, walkoff home run in the bottom of the ninth to win Game 4 of the 2001 American League Championship Series. After Tino Martinez tied Game 4 of the 2001 World Series with a dramatic ninth inning two-run home run, Derek Jeter ended the contest with a line drive into the right field seats in the bottom of the 10th inning.

Soriano won Game 5 of the Series with a walkoff RBI single in the bottom of the 12th inning. Mark Teixeira had his "Yankee moment" in Game 2 of the American League Divisional Series vs. the Minnesota Twins. In the bottom of the 11th inning, "Tex" slammed a line drive into the left field stands that went just inside the foul pole for a game-winning home run.

In Game 3 of the 2012 American League Divisional Series against Baltimore, Yankees designated hitter Raul Ibanez tied the game in the ninth inning with a home run, and then won the game with another homer in the 12th inning.

Jerry Coleman had a walkoff RBI single in Game 3 of the 1950 World Series against the Philadelphia Phillies. In

1953, Billy Martin's walkoff RBI single in the bottom of the 9th inning of Game 6 against the Brooklyn Dodgers ended the game and the World Series. In the 1977 and 1978 World Series against the Los Angeles Dodgers, Paul Blair and Lou Piniella had extra-inning walkoff hits. Blair's hit won Game 1 in the 12th inning. Piniella ended Game 4 with a walkoff RBI single in the bottom of the 10th to even the Series at two games apiece. Second baseman Jose Vizcaino ended Game 1 of the 2000 World Series with a walkoff RBI single in the bottom of the 12th inning. The Yankees have played in 225 World Series games. No Yankees pitcher has ever hit a World Series home run.

10. The Yankees and Boston Red Sox have had a long history of memorable regular season games.

One of the most famous was an extra-inning epic that took place at Yankee Stadium on July 1, 2004. This game is remembered for Yankees shortstop Derek Jeter diving into the stands to make a remarkable play, but it was also one of the most exciting regular season games between the two rivals. The game was tied at 3 when Boston had a golden opportunity to break the tie in the top of the 11th. The Red Sox had the bases loaded and no one out against Mariano Rivera. Boston right fielder Kevin Millar hit a grounder toward the third base line. Alex Rodriguez went to his knees right over the bag to field the ball, record the out at third, and throw home to complete a 5–2 double play and prevent the go-ahead run from scoring. Rivera got the final out to keep the game tied at that point.

In the top of the 12th, the Red Sox had runners at second and third with two out. Pinch-hitter Trot Nixon lifted a pop fly that drifted toward the left field line and looked as though it was going to drop in. Jeter raced over and caught the ball in fair territory, but could not stop his momentum. Once he reached the stands, the Yankee shortstop braced himself and then dove head first into the lower box seats. When he emerged from the crowd around him, his face was bloodied and he had a nasty bruise under his right eye and chin. Jeter was due up in the bottom of the 12th, but Jason Giambi pinch-hit for him. With one out and the winning run at third, he struck out swinging.

Red Sox relief pitcher Curtis Leskanic hit Gary Sheffield with a pitch and Alex Rodriguez was intentionally walked to load the bases with one out. After a forceout at home, Bernie Williams struck out to end the inning.

In the top of the 13th, Rodriguez moved to shortstop (for one of only five times he ever played there in his career as a Yankee) and Sheffield went to third base (one of only two times he played that position in his Yankees career).

Noted "Yankees killer" Manny Ramirez led off the 13th inning with a home run to give the Red Sox a 4–3 lead.

Leskanic got the first two outs of the 13th inning relatively easily, striking out Jorge Posada and dispensing with Tony Clark on a bouncer back to the mound. Right fielder Ruben Sierra kept the game alive with a two-out single to center. Second baseman Miguel Cairo lined a 1–2 pitch into the gap in right-center field to score Sierra with the tying run. A pinch-hitter, backup catcher John Flaherty, hit a 3–1 pitch into the left field corner to score Cairo with the winning run for a thrilling 5–4 win.

There was some confusion as to whether Flaherty was credited with a single or a ground rule double after the ball bounced into the left field seats. Flaherty rounded first and pumped his fist, but never went to second.

According to the scoring rules in baseball's *Official Rule Book*, since Cairo was on second and could score on a two-out single, combined with the fact that Flaherty never touched second, it went in the box score as a single.

Cairo was a journeyman player who played for nine teams and spent parts of three seasons with the Yankees. Flaherty played the final three seasons of his 14-year career with the Yankees, from 2003 to 2005.

Surprisingly, Jeter played the next night in an interleague game against the New York Mets at Shea Stadium. He had earlier made another famous play in the 2001 American League Divisional Series against the Oakland Athletics. The A's won the first two games at Yankee Stadium, so The Bronx Bombers were on the ropes going into Game 3 in Oakland. Starter Mike Mussina was pitching a brilliant game and the Yankees led 1–0 in the bottom of the seventh. With two out, A's designated hitter Jeremy Giambi singled. Oakland's Terence Long lined a double into the right field corner, which is spacious at the Oakland Coliseum. It appeared that Giambi was going to come around and score the tying run. Yankees right fielder Shane Spencer played the ball down the right field line and threw it back in. Jeter somehow anticipated that Spencer's relay would miss the cutoff man, so he darted toward the first base line to play the ball. In a play that came to be known as "the flip," Jeter backhanded the ball to Posada. For some reason, Giambi did not elect to slide and that allowed the Yankees catcher to put the tag on him to end the inning.

The Yankees won that game, 1–0, and eventually rallied to take the Series in five games.

Sources

Books

162–0: Imagine a Perfect Yankees Season, Marty Appel. (Chicago, Triumph Books, 2010)

Core Four: The Heart and Soul of the Yankees Dynasty, Phil Pepe. (Chicago, Triumph Books, 2013)

DiMaggio, Setting the Record Straight, Morris Engelberg and Marv Schneider. (Minneapolis, Motorbooks International, 2003)

Great Hitters of the Negro Leagues, Paul Hoblin. (New York, Sportszone, 2012)

Yankees Essential: Everything You Need to Know to Be a Real Fan, Howie Karpin. (Chicago, Triumph Books, 2007)

Periodicals and websites

Associated Press
New York Times
New York Yankees 2016 Official Media Guide and Record Book
baseball-reference.com
moregehrig.tripod.com
sabr.org
themick.com

Acknowledgments

As has been a tradition, I begin with thanking my family for their support, including my wonderful wife, Kathy, and my two boys, Danny and Jake; my sister, Carol Shore, her husband, Barry, and my nieces, Wendy and Sharon and their families.

Larry Fleischer was a big help in supplementing my list of questions, and I thank him for his assistance.

Thanks to my "right hand" man at Mets games, Bob Waterman of Elias, for his help.

Of course, thanks to Niels Aaboe of Skyhorse for believing in me with this project and previous works that I've been a part of.

Finally, thanks to Ken Samelson, my longtime friend who got me started with writing books, and who is my "publishing guru."